Implementing an Information Security Management System

Security Management Based on ISO 27001 Guidelines

Abhishek Chopra
Mukund Chaudhary

Apress®

Implementing an Information Security Management System

Abhishek Chopra
Faridabad, Haryana, India

Mukund Chaudhary
Noida, India

ISBN-13 (pbk): 978-1-4842-5412-7
https://doi.org/10.1007/978-1-4842-5413-4

ISBN-13 (electronic): 978-1-4842-5413-4

Managing Director, Apress Media LLC: Welmoed Spahr
Acquisitions Editor: Nikhil Karkal
Development Editor: Matthew Moodie
Coordinating Editor: Divya Modi

Cover designed by eStudioCalamar

Cover image designed by Pixabay

Distributed to the book trade worldwide by Springer Science+Business Media New York, 233 Spring Street, 6th Floor, New York, NY 10013. Phone 1-800-SPRINGER, fax (201) 348-4505, e-mail orders-ny@springer-sbm.com, or visit www.springeronline.com. Apress Media, LLC is a California LLC and the sole member (owner) is Springer Science + Business Media Finance Inc (SSBM Finance Inc). SSBM Finance Inc is a **Delaware** corporation.

For information on translations, please e-mail rights@apress.com, or visit http://www.apress.com/rights-permissions.

Apress titles may be purchased in bulk for academic, corporate, or promotional use. eBook versions and licenses are also available for most titles. For more information, reference our Print and eBook Bulk Sales web page at http://www.apress.com/bulk-sales.

Any source code or other supplementary material referenced by the author in this book is available to readers on GitHub via the book's product page, located at www.apress.com/978-1-4842-5412-7. For more detailed information, please visit http://www.apress.com/source-code.

Printed on acid-free paper

*This book is dedicated to my grandfather,
the late Kameshwar Chaudhary*

Table of Contents

About the Authors

 **Abhishek Chopra** is a quality professional with more than 14 years of experience implementing CMMi, ISO 9001, ITIL, and ISO 27001. He holds a black belt in Lean Six Sigma and is a certified ISO 27001 lead auditor.

 **Mukund Chaudhary** is a certified project management professional with more than a decade of experience in managing software projects, internal audits, CMMI, and ISO 27001. In his leisure time, he can be found reading articles and exploring emerging technologies.

About the Technical Reviewer

Dominic Fernandes is a seasoned and highly experienced veteran of the information systems architecture and security arena, he has worked with leading edge technologies in challenging environments in various global and multinational industries.

Among his strengths are IS audits, project management, team building, and organizational strategy.

Dominic Fernandes is an avid reader of varied content, ranging from leading edge technology to biographies and economy. He loves and appreciates music and languages across cultures and is a nature lover and environmentalist.

Acknowledgments

I would like to thank all the special people below.

My older sister, Meenakshi Chopra, guided my career path, introduced me to the field of information security, and taught me its importance. My brother-in-law, Rajasekaran Stanley, has been a great support and has always encouraged me to do new things.

Heartfelt respect for my dear friend and brotherly figure Mukund Chaudhary, who inspired me to write my experiences in this book. Special thanks to my mother, Anita Chopra, who is my number one guide and a true inspiration to me. To my colleagues and friends, Anushka and Suchee, thank you for encouraging me and always sharing your best wishes.

Finally, thank you to the editors for their aspiring guidance and friendly advice, especially Divya Modi and Nikhil Karkal.

—*Abhishek Chopra*

I would like to thank my organization, which gave me the opportunity to take ownership of the ISO 27001 implementation and supported me with training. I'd also like to express my gratitude to everyone who supported me while I was writing this book. I am thankful to the editors for their inspiring guidance and friendly advice, especially to Nikhil Karkal and Divya Modi.

I would also like to thank all my colleagues and friends for their support. I sincerely thank everyone, including my parents, my wife Nandita, and my friends and teammates who encouraged me to write. Special thanks to my grandfather, the late Kameshwar Chaudhary, who always inspired me to write.

—*Mukund Chaudhary*

Introduction

Thank you very much for purchasing this book legally. Information security professionals have access to confidential data that belongs to the organization and, therefore, they must possess high ethical standards.

This book begins by discussing the need for information security and accessing the need and scope of the audit. Most of us do not know where to start the implementation in our organizations; hence this book will help guide you step by step. The book covers initial risk assessment and the risk management approach. The controls are each explained in detail so as to make the implementation easy, even for novice readers, per the ISO 27001 standard. The book also covers audit requirements, explains how to conduct the audits, and discusses how to close the gaps/findings.

This book discusses the process of conducting management reviews and best practices to manage and close the audit. Finally, it focuses on continual improvement of the organization's information security system.

Who This Book Is For

This book is for security professionals who want to implement and manage security framework/controls within their organization. For example, it's for security managers, IT consultants, IT auditors, management professionals, and anybody else who inspires to work as a security professional. This includes beginners who are seeking to gain knowledge about information security concepts. Anybody with very basic knowledge of security concepts can learn from this book. It does not require expertise with security tools.

The book is organized in such a way that beginners with no prior security experience will also get good insights into the audit cycle. Each chapter has a specific purpose; however, you can skip chapters and read only the ones that meet your needs. For example, if you already know why information security is needed, feel free to move to the next chapter. However, for best results, we do not recommend skipping chapters.

Some of you may have already completed an audit in your organization and you want to focus more on post-audit activities. In that case, we recommend you read all the tips shared in the "Management Review" and "Continual Improvement" chapters (Chapters 8 and 10).

CHAPTER 1

The Need for Information Security

In theory, one can build provably secure systems. In theory, theory can be applied to practice but in practice, it can't.

—M. Dacier, Eurecom Institute

This chapter lays the foundation for understanding information security. It discusses the following:

- What is information security?

- Information security management ISO 27001

- Why is it important to safeguard information?

- How is the ISO 27001 applicable to you?

What Is Information Security?

Before you learn about information security and see how important it is, you first need to understand terms like *information* and *security*.

When you see these two words—information and security—you might wonder what type of information is being discussed and why you would need to secure it.

The truth is that people unknowingly do many things that put their personal information at risk and they often don't know the impact of this mistake.

© Abhishek Chopra, Mukund Chaudhary 2020
A. Chopra and M. Chaudhary, *Implementing an Information Security Management System*,
https://doi.org/10.1007/978-1-4842-5413-4_1

Securing information is a big challenge. This includes not only the protection of your personal information but also of organizations that store your personal information on their systems. We give organizations our consent to keep our information and they have the responsibility to protect it from getting into the wrong hands.

In addition, an organization's information could be stolen by their competitors. Industries that are particularly vulnerable include the banking, automobile, aviation, software, and hardware industries.

The type of information that you need to secure includes personal and organizational data.

Personal information includes banking data like ATM card details, transaction details, information regarding banking passwords, and other personal details. Medical reports are also at risk of being stolen—this can be in the form of electronic reports or hard copies.

Organizational data, such as trade secrets, product designs, and customer information, is also at risk and must be secured.

There are various ways and means to protect information. In this book, you will learn about the various best practices. To explain these best practices, the book uses the ISO 27001 information security standard, which is recognized internationally.

The following section discusses data and information, so you have a broader understanding of information security.

Data

Data can be any raw fact used to make decisions. Data is defined as a group of numbers, letters, special characters in the form of text, images, voice recordings, and so on. For example, the number 1034778 could be a bank account number, an enrollment number at a university, a vehicle number, and so on. The number in this example is just raw fact and hence it's called *data*.

Information

Information is data that can be processed to provide meaning. Information can be related data that enables you to make decisions. In other words, information brings clarity to the data so that you can act on it.

As per the definition given by Davis and Olson:

Information is data that has been processed into a form that is meaningful to the recipient and is of real or perceived value in current or prospective actions or decisions.

Figure 1-1 shows that information is processed data that gives users meaningful conclusions.

Figure 1-1. *How data is processed to get information*

Note   We are living in an age in which we deal with lots of information on a daily basis, but we care most about the information that is relevant to us.

Here are some characteristics of information:

- *Availability:* The information is available when required. For example, if you need some back-dated data that you saved on the cloud a few years ago, it should be available when required.

- *Accuracy:* The information is correct. The decisions that you make are based on the accuracy of the information. For example, an experienced team member estimates the project's timeline and your budget is allocated based on that information. If the information is not correct, that may lead to project delays or even termination.

- *Authenticity:* This term refers to the originality of the information. It should not have been altered by anyone else. For example, if you are presenting a status report to your client, it should be authentic or original.

- *Confidentiality:* Only those people who have access rights or are authorized can see the information. For example, salary data is confidential, so only authorized persons should be able to access that information.

- *Integrity:* Integrity refers to the completeness of the information. The information that you save must be complete and not corrupted. For example, you save important information to the database. When you access it, it must be retrieved the same way it was saved.

Information security is the practice of protecting information from unauthorized use. We are living in an era where electronic devices such as laptops and mobile phones have become part of our basic needs. We save huge amounts of information on our computers, smartphones, storage devices, tablets, and on paper and then we often treat them as ordinary files that have no importance.

But if this information gets into the wrong hands, it can lead to inconvenience, monetary losses, and reputation issues for the organization. Hence, you need to make sure that all your important documents are password protected, and you should avoid the habit of using the same passwords for everything.

Information security is not only about securing information against unauthorized access. It is the practice of preventing unauthorized access, use, modification, and destruction of information.

Let's now look at why a standard on information security was necessary. You should know the basic history and origin of information security.

How ISO 27001 Applies to You

Imagine you are responsible for securing confidential data. What if this information was stolen? What if your competitor accessed this information? In the wrong hands, personal information can be used against you. This section explains how ISO 27001 can safeguard your information.

ISO 27001: Information Security Management System

The BSI (British Standards Institution) Group originally published the standard called BS 7799. It was written by the United Kingdom government's Department of Trade and Industry (DTI) and consisted of several parts.

The first part, containing the best practices for information security management, was revised in 1998. It was adopted in 2000 by the ISO as ISO/IEC 17799, titled "Information Technology: Code of Practice for Information Security Management". ISO/IEC 17799 was then revised in June 2005 and incorporated into the ISO 27000 series of standards as ISO/IEC 27002 in July 2007.

The second part of the standard BS 7799 was published in 1999 with the title "Information Security Management System". The focus of BS 7799-2 was on how to implement an information security management system. Later, this was updated to cover risk analysis and management and was called ISO/IEC 27001:2005.

The latest published version of the Information Security Management System (ISMS) standard is BS EN ISO/IEC 27001: 2017. The ISO version of the standard (2013) was not affected by the 2017 publication and the changes do not introduce any new requirements. If you are interested in reading a detailed history of information security, read BS 7799-3:2017.

An ISMS is a framework of policies and procedures for ameliorating risk.

- *Define an information security policy:* The main purpose of an information security policy is to define what top management wants to achieve with its security measures. This tells management who is responsible for which items, with clear expectations, roles, and responsibilities.

- *Define the scope of ISMS:* Scope is an important factor in accordance with the statement of applicability. The scope should cover the location of the information security audit, the functions involved in the audit, as well as the personnel and assets involved (physical, software, and information). It should clearly define any exclusions. For example, say you are performing an audit for a software division that includes the HR, IT, and admin departments (not including sales and marketing). In this case, your scope document should clearly define sales and marketing as exclusions.

- *Conduct a risk assessment:* Risk assessment is an essential part of any business and ISO 27001 focuses on risk-based planning. The assessment or analysis is based on the asset register. In simple words, you need to identify which incidents might happen and determine the best way to do asset-based risk assessments. This can be done by creating a focus group, holding a brainstorming session, or interviewing asset owners.

- *Manage identified risks:* When managing identified risks, it is important to use the plan document. When a risk is identified, it should be registered into the risk register and categorized based on the organizational risk management plan. The asset owners should be responsible for their asset risk; however, the standard does not tell you how to deal with the risk.

- *Select the control objectives and controls to be implemented:* There is a long list of controls in ISO 27001. Chapter 7 covers these controls in detail.

- *Prepare a statement of applicability:* A statement of applicability in ISO 27001 is also referred to as an *SOA document.* It is one of the most important documents in the system and organizations generally tend to spend more time preparing it. This document will tell you how they implement the controls. It also identifies any inclusions and exclusions.

This international standard provides requirements for establishing, implementing, maintaining, and continually improving an information security management system. An ISMS is a systematic approach to managing sensitive company information so that it remains secure.

Adopting an ISMS is a strategic decision since it includes people, processes, and IT systems. It can help small, medium, and large businesses in any sector keep their assets secure.

If you are new to ISO 27001 and are familiar with some other standard, you may assume that by purchasing/downloading the standard, you can figure out what you need to do, but that is not the case.

ISO 27001 is not prescriptive. It doesn't tell you what kind of technology to use to protect your network or how often you need to perform backups, for example. Those decisions need to be made by your organization.

Imagine if the standard prescribed that you needed to back up your system every 24 hours. How do you know that this is the right interval for your organization? Organizations have different needs and different types and amounts of data.

For example, companies like Facebook, Google, LinkedIn, etc. generate petabytes of data every day. The rate of change of their data is very quick and they need real-time backup (or if not real-time, at least hourly backup). Conversely, there are small organizations for which the rate of data change is very slow. Their backup interval could easily be once a week.

Note   Facebook generates four new petabytes of data and runs 600,000 queries and 1 million MapReduce jobs per day. Source: `https://research.fb.com/`.

ISMSs stand on three main pillars, referred to as the CIA triad (see Figure 1-2):

- Confidentiality
- Integrity
- Availability

Confidentiality

Confidentiality refers to protecting information from being accessed by unauthorized parties. Imagine that you started a new company. You have physical assets like a building, equipment, and computers. You have employees and important data, which are also assets. You want only authorized people to see the data, so you want to implement confidentiality. This way, only authorized people can access the data and work with it. You can implement confidentiality by encrypting the data files and then storing them to a disk. By doing this, only people who have access to the disk can see the data and work with it.

In terms of personal information, say you want to open a new savings account at the bank and need to invest $10,000. This information is confidential, as only the bank and you can access it.

Integrity

Integrity refers to the consistency, accuracy, and trustworthiness of data over its entire lifecycle. If you transfer $1001 to your friend, you want to be sure that he receives $1001. You want to be confident that an unauthorized attacker can't alter or manipulate it to make it $100, or that the bank won't make an error.

Availability

The availability of data is also very important. If the data is stored in a database, it is very important that the business or authorized user can access it when needed. The data should be readily available to authorized users. If the data is secured but not available when it's requested, this can be a big risk to the company. Say you go to the bank to withdraw some money from your account, but the bank official tells you that service is not available at that time. You will likely lose faith in that bank. Availability is ensured by continuously maintaining the hardware and software. It is important to ensure an optimal environment that is free from software conflicts. Security equipment, such as firewalls and proxy servers, can guard against downtime and ensure protection from denial of service (DoS) attacks.

Figure 1-2. *The CIA triad*

Why Is It Important to Safeguard Information?

Safeguarding information is essential to protecting yourself and your organization against malicious or misguided attacks. As examples of what can happen when your data is not secure, this section describes some real security breaches that happened in the past. These examples will help you understand the following:

- What the motive was and what kind of information was stolen

- What the impact was

- How the security breach happened

Yahoo

Year: 2013-14

Impact: 3 billion user accounts

Yahoo announced that a state-sponsored actor pulled off a big data breach in 2014. This breach included the real names, email addresses, dates of birth, and telephone numbers of 500 million users. Most of the passwords were hashed using a robust encryption algorithm.

Marriott International

Year: 2014-18

Impact: 500 million customers

In November 2018, Marriott International announced that cybercriminals had stolen 500 million customers' data. Marriott had acquired the Starwood hotel in 2016, and the cyberthieves had attacked and entered their system. This was not discovered until September 2018.

In this attack, 100 million customers' credit card numbers and expiration dates were stolen. For some, only their names and contact information were taken. Marriott communicated that they believed the attackers were not able to decrypt the credit card numbers.

According to *The New York Times* published article, a Chinese intelligence group pulled off that attack.

eBay

Year: May 2014

Impact: 145 million users compromised

In May 2014, eBay reported a cyberattack in which all of its 145 million users' personal details were stolen. That included their names, addresses, dates of birth, and encrypted passwords. How did this happen? The hackers used the credentials of eBay employees to enter the company network. They had complete access to the user database for more than seven months.

When eBay discovered this breach, they requested its users change their passwords, and they communicated that the users' credit card numbers were not stolen, as they were stored separately.

Heartland Payment Systems

Year: March 2008

Impact: 134 million credit cards exposed through SQL injection to install spyware on Heartland's data systems

In January 2009, Visa and MasterCard reported suspicious transactions to Heartland payment systems. At that time, Heartland was processing over 100 million payment card transactions per month.

Heartland was declared non-compliant by the Payment Card Industry Data Security Standard (PCI DSS). That meant that major credit card providers were not allowed to process their payments. This ban was in place until May 2009. They were also asked to pay an estimated $145 million in compensation for fraudulent payments.

It was discovered that two unnamed Russians masterminded the international operation that stole the credit and debit cards. This all happened due to a vulnerability of many web-facing applications which made SQL injection the most common form of attack against websites.

Uber

Year: Late 2016

Impact: Personal information of 57 million Uber users and 600,000 drivers exposed

In late 2016, Uber discovered that a hacker had stolen the names, email addresses, and mobile phone numbers of 57 million users of their app. The driver license numbers of 600,000 Uber drivers were also stolen. Hackers also stole usernames and password credentials to Uber's AWS account by getting access to their GitHub account.

Uber had to pay the hackers $100,000 to destroy the data. It cost Uber in terms of reputation and money.

Note   The source of this security breach was published on the csonline blog at `https://www.csoonline.com/article/2130877/the-biggest-data-breaches-of-the-21st-century.html`.

NHS Cyberattack

Year: May 2017

Impact: WannaCry crippled 200,000 computers with a message demanding cryptocurrency in bitcoin. This attack resulted in about $112 million in losses.

Hackers broadcasted ransomware called WannaCry, also called WanaCrypt, through emails that tricked the recipients into opening the attachments and releasing malware onto their systems. Once the system was affected, it encrypted the files and locked it in such a manner that users could not access it. Then a red message was displayed demanding payment in cryptocurrency bitcoin in order to regain access.

Hospitals and GP surgeries in the UK were hit by this ransomware attack. The hospital staff had no option other than to use pen, paper, and their own mobile phones when the attack affected key systems, including telephones and other important equipment. This forced the hospitals to cancel appointments, which resulted in huge losses.

The attackers blackmailed the healthcare systems without any assurance that access would be granted after the payment was done.

Safeguarding Summary

After reading these real-life scenarios, you can see where information security may apply to you and your organization. You learned that you need to reduce or eliminate the risks related to unauthorized disclosure, modification, and deletion of critical information.

Industry-wide information security can be applicable to any industry. There is a myth about information security being applicable only to the software or IT industries. The fact is that any industry that generates information that's valuable to them needs good information security.

Scenario 1: Banking

Banking transactions are part of our day-to-day activities and most people have one or more savings accounts. According to the Global Findex World Bank report, 69 percent of adults have an account, up from 62 percent in 2014 and 51 percent in 2011.

India saw a major rise in account numbers after the announcement of PM Narendra Modi's "Jan Dhan" scheme. The total number of savings accounts rose to 1.57 billion in March 2017, compared to 1.22 billion in 2015.

The numbers clearly show that banking is integral to our daily life and hence securing that data is a continuous challenge. The good news is that with emerging technologies, we can keep our data secure if we follow the guidelines and standard procedures.

If a bank does not secure important information like account details, account balances, and transaction histories, its customers would lose trust in it and may not feel safe depositing money there.

As a personal example, imagine you ran into one of your friends after a long time and she asked for your phone or cell number. You would probably feel comfortable exchanging this information, since she is your friend. But what if she asked for your credit card number and CVV pin? You should be willing to share only things that are not confidential. The same goes with banks. Your account number is yours only and only you are supposed to get the details of your account by authenticating your identity.

If you are using a mobile banking application, you understand that your customer ID and password are highly confidential and sharing them with others is like sharing the key to your home and valuables. Some countries do not require two-factor authentication, but others require you to enter your high security code, which is one-time password (OTP) received on your registered mobile number. This gives you the assurance that your transactions are more secure.

Cybersecurity is of utmost importance in the financial/banking sector. The foundation of the banking system lies in nurturing trust and credibility. In this digital age, people seem to be going cashless, instead using digital currencies like crypto-currencies such as bitcoin, debit cards, credit cards, and wallet payments. In this context, it becomes very important for banks to ensure all measures of cybersecurity, to protect your money and your privacy.

For financial institutions such as banks, data breaches can result in serious trust issues. A weak cybersecurity system can lead to data breaches that could easily cause the customer base to take its money elsewhere.

Even in the case of a minor information leak, banks need have to cancel the previously issued card, dispatch a new card, and then monitor accounts for similar incidents.

Banks are responsible for guarding the financial data of their customers and for keeping their operations safe. Banks are prone to security breaches if they are not protected from cybercrime.

These days, people do lots of financial transactions via online banking and ATM machines. Both of these must be very secure. Banks therefore make a lot of effort to safeguard online transactions and data from hackers.

ATM machines are an important part of the banking system and must be secure. There are cases in which the ATM card slot was compromised. This is a high-tech form of theft from ATM machines called *skimming*. Thieves place a card reader over the real ATM card slot. When you slide your card into the card slot, the reader captures all your information and later they can clone the card to steal your hard-earned money.

Cosmos Bank Cyberattack

Impact of the attack: $13.5 million stolen from the Cosmos Bank

Scope: ATM switch compromise, swift environment compromise, and malware infection

According to cyber experts, the attacker hacked the ATM switch of the Cosmos Bank to access the firewall server. Figure 1-3 shows an overview of how an ATM switch works.

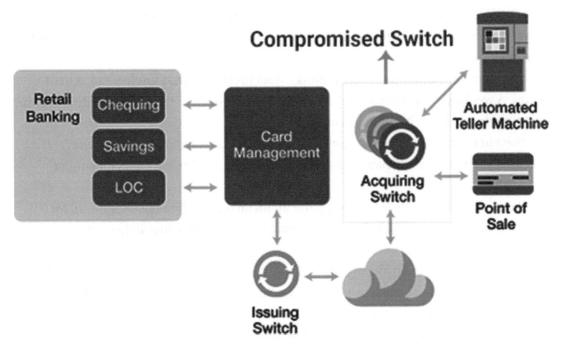

Figure 1-3. *Switch architecture*

Whenever you do any transactions like change your PIN or withdraw money, the ATM switch authenticates the transaction. When you do transactions using a different bank's ATM card, the ATM switch verifies that the card is the original card issued by the bank and it belongs to you.

In the case of the Cosmos cyberattack, the hackers bypassed the firewall of the ATM switch and performed self-authorized transactions by using a proxy server that they created.

The attackers directly connected to the bank's server and performed approximately 12,000 transactions using a Visa debit card. The bank was unaware of the false transactions for two days.

According to the report available from the Maharashtra Special Investigation Team, who investigated the attack, they have not been able to link the attack to any group, since the attacker wiped out all tracks, leaving no evidence of the incident.

Scenario 2: Trade Secrets

We all are aware of Apple and the iPhone. Imagine if you are an Apple employee and are working in the product design department. You have the access to the new iPhone designs before their launch. If this information gets leaked to the outside world, imagine the impact on the company and on the morale of the employees.

Management may feel mistrustful of the employees, thinking that they are the origin of this breach. The outside world may be concerned that the company cannot protect its confidential data. This can have a major impact on company revenue and on the product image. Competitors get to see the new design and might be able to release a similar look-alike product before the launch of the original product at a cheaper price.

It becomes important to protect the product information throughout its lifecycle, from its concept/design phase to the product release phase.

Information security was and always will be a challenge. Apple has been affected by serious security issues many times. In 2014, the company's iCloud data storage was hit by a flurry of apparent breaches, culminating in a targeted attack on celebrity accounts. This was dubbed Celebgate. In this attack, various embarrassing images of Hollywood celebrities and actors were leaked to the Internet. In short, if you are storing personal data on cloud services, you should know that it is not 100% safe. Better not to store any personal and sensitive data on the cloud. For example, if you saved an Excel file on your mobile or laptop that's highly confidential, you need to keep it password protected.

Scenario 3: Healthcare

Healthcare is one the sector in which awareness about security is low. Hackers try attack systems that are less secure and more easily prone to compromise. Cybercriminals can easily trap hospital data, as it is often less secure. You might wonder what kind of data one can get from a hospital. The answer is social security numbers (SSN), names of the patient, companies they are insured with, their blood types, and so on. This kind of information can be very handy for criminals.

They can get more details and interlinked information from your SSN or Aadhar card, if you are from India. Again, your confidential information, like credit card details if you happen to pay through that medium, are all exposed. More innocuous information can serve as the first step to steal confidential information that otherwise you would not share.

According to the PwC Healthcare research institute, the consequences of a data breach in a hospital can be up to $200 per patient, while the cost of prevention is just $8 per patient. The famous quote by Desiderius Erasmus, "prevention is better than cure," comes to mind here. It fits well with cybersecurity. Some of the leading healthcare organizations are now investing in information security. So, will the ISO 27001 standard be enough to protect the healthcare industry?

It can help healthcare organizations, but if you want to implement additional healthcare directives pertaining to the healthcare domain, you may choose ISO 27799.

Table 1-1. *Directives Provided in ISO 27799 (Section 6) But Not Stated in the ISO 27001*

ISO 27799 Subsection	Summary of Additional Directives Pertaining to the Healthcare Domain as Provided in the ISO 27799
6.4.3	A unique forum called an information security management forum (ISMF) should be established to manage and direct the information security management system activities within the healthcare sector. When organizing the ISMF within the healthcare sector, stakeholder views need to be accommodated and regulatory obligations are to be met.
	A scope statement may be used in various types of organizations, but in the case of health organizations, the scope statement should be publicized widely, reviewed, and adopted by the organization's information, clinical and corporate governance groups. Some health organizations seek comments on the scope statement from clinicians' professional regulatory bodies, which may be aware of other organizations pursuing compliance or certification.
6.4.4.2	Information security risk assessment is important in the healthcare sector because the sector carries high risk due to having facilities such as laboratories, emergency departments and operating theatres. Both qualitative and quantitative factors need to be considered when assessing information security risks in these environments. Examples of issues to consider when designing valuation guidelines are recognizing the importance of patient safety; uninterrupted availability of emergency services; professional accreditation; and clinical regulation.

(continued)

Table 1-1. (*continued*)

ISO 27799 Subsection	Summary of Additional Directives Pertaining to the Healthcare Domain as Provided in the ISO 27799
6.4.4.4	Information custodianship, ownership, and responsibility are issues that are raised when risk assessment is to be undertaken in the healthcare sector. For effective information security risk assessment to be achieved in the healthcare sector, the knowledge and skills listed below are necessary: a) Clinical and nursing process knowledge, including care protocols and pathways b) Knowledge of the formats of clinical data and the capability for the misuse of this data c) Knowledge of external environment factors that could exacerbate or moderate any or all the levels of the risk components described previously d) Information on IT and medical device attributes and performance/failure characteristics e) Knowledge of incident histories and actual case impact scenarios f) Detailed knowledge of systems architectures g) Familiarity with change management programs that would change any or all the risk component levels
6.4.5.3	There are numerous factors to be considered to define criteria for the acceptance of risks. A selection from these factors includes: a) Health sector, industry or organizational standards b) Clinical or other priorities c) Cultural fit d) Reactions of subjects of care (patients) e) Coherence with IT, clinical, and corporate risk acceptance strategy
6.4.6	The organization's information security officer, data protection officer or risk manager should be responsible for the security improvement plan of the organization on behalf of the ISMF. The plans should be made available to clinical and other staff; they are useful in demonstrating progress and process improvement. These plans are sometimes effective in minimizing interruptions to operations when integrated with information security improvement, planned changes in IT facilities and healthcare.

(*continued*)

Table 1-1. (*continued*)

ISO 27799 Subsection	Summary of Additional Directives Pertaining to the Healthcare Domain as Provided in the ISO 27799
6.5	Because of the critical nature of health information systems, it is especially important to define responsibilities and action steps in the initial phase of response because events can unfold quickly, and this leaves little time for reflection as a security incident unfolds.
	In the health context the ISMF is further responsible for making sure that the risk treatment plan is carried out. In healthcare approving the risk treatment plan may involve both information governance and clinical governance.

Note   If you work in the healthcare domain and have further interest in this topic, check out https://www.iso.org/obp/ui/#iso:std:iso:27799:ed-2:v1:en

Scenario 4: Manufacturing

The manufacturing industry is no different than other industries when it comes to vulnerability. Attackers are targeting manufacturers in order to steal information about new products, processes, or technologies that the manufacturer creates. This can be a secret formula, blueprints of confidential designs, or any process. For example, a competitor try to steal the magic formula or unique ingredients for his new noodle business in order to sell products at a lower price and reduce the margins and competitive edge.

The operation technology used by manufacturers is very often unsecured and therefore vulnerable to external cyberattacks and internal threats. Attackers know that manufacturers' networks can be easily compromised because of the lack of awareness of cybersecurity tools and processes.

The following sections look at some real-world examples of manufacturing threats. These real-world cases will help you understand the potential consequences for the manufacturing industry.

Stuxnet Virus

In 2011, the Stuxnet worm targeted the PLC system of Iran's nuclear program and destroyed many of its nuclear centrifuges. This virus is said to be one of the most successful industrial attacks in cyber history.

At the time of this writing, no data was available to show the impact in terms of revenue. But the attack successfully destroyed a fifth of Iran's nuclear centrifuges and damaged the country's nuclear program quite badly.

Scenario 5: Information Technology

This scenario considers people who work with software development companies or are aware of how the industry operates. The software company develops software applications/products for their external and internal customers. The company receives a lot of information in terms of requirements from their clients and these are highly confidential. They can be considered the intellectual property of the customer, especially if the product/application is not available in the market yet.

It becomes very important for the company to safeguard this information. That's why many companies require non-disclosure agreements (NDA) to be signed. Both parties officially agree not to disclose information to another third party.

An NDA creates a confidential relationship between the parties, in order to protect confidential and proprietary information or trade secrets. Once both companies agree and start working together, we call it a *project* and assign a team to it.

Note   A *project* is a temporary endeavor having a definite start and end date. Projects must be aligned to organizational goals and should be executed in a secure environment.

Upon assigning team members to the project, they must be reminded of their responsibilities to safeguard client information. They should never disclose that information to unauthorized persons or to anyone outside the organization.

Consider how the information will be used and accessed during the project execution and all the ways it needs to be safeguarded.

As part of the project, team members need to prepare or access many documents and work on the source code repository. The project manager, with the help of the IT team, must define and provide access for each team member working on the project. Members access is usually defined as read, write, and delete. Only a few privileged members can delete information. This may be a part of the configuration control and the role may vary depending on the organization.

It is also important to review the access rights on a regular basis. IT teams who provide access to the source code repository must keep track of users, in order to stop any unauthorized access or tampering with the information. For example, a team member may try to send client information outside the official email system to their personal email or other known contacts. Also, if USB ports are not disabled, it becomes very easy to copy and transfer information to a USB stick and carry it outside.

Once the project is delivered, the client might ask to have the source code (developed by the company for the client), which must then be deleted from company systems. This is to ensure that the company doesn't reuse that source code for its benefit.

Summary

The most important point of this chapter is that information security is critical. The impact of having your personal or organizational information stolen could be devastating; it's important to safeguard it.

This chapter also discussed who is responsible for information security—the answer is everybody is responsible! You are responsible for protecting your own information, and, in an organization, it becomes important that every employee understand his responsibility to protect the organization and client information.

This chapter covered a few examples to explain how information security is applicable in different industries. You should now also understand that there is no one way to safeguard information. You may need various controls and checks in place to do so. You will learn more about this in the upcoming chapters that cover ISO 27001 security controls.

The next chapter discusses various aspects of the implementation process and how to start it.

CHAPTER 2

Assessing Needs and Scope

BYOD must evolve from 'Bring Your Own Devil' to 'Bring Your Own Defense' associated to security probation and monitoring.

—Stéphane Nappo

Nearly all industries and organizations rely on computers to do their daily tasks, regardless of the industry they're in, which means the security of digital information has become of upmost importance.

Organizations generate lots of business-critical information and no organization can keep up without that data. When planning to implement ISO 27001, the first step is to assess the business's needs and scope.

To start an ISO 27001 implementation, you must first understand the business context of your organization. Why is your organization going for ISO 27001 certification? The decision to implement ISO 27001 can be a strategic one driven from upper management and the way you are taking it can be different.

Assessing Business Needs

Once the business need is clear, you can implement a robust ISMS (Information Security Management System) that covers the needs of the interested parties and customers. It should also meet management expectations.

Clause 4.1 of ISO 27001, identifying the organizational context, is the first step in implementation. This clause requires you to analyze the external and internal issues that influence your company's information security.

© Abhishek Chopra, Mukund Chaudhary 2020
A. Chopra and M. Chaudhary, *Implementing an Information Security Management System*,
https://doi.org/10.1007/978-1-4842-5413-4_2

It is important to understand the external and internal environments affecting the company when you're defining an ISMS. The ISO standard for information security management requires that you define the organizational context.

As per ISO 31000 Clause 5.3.1, these issues can be of two types:

- *Internal issues:* Factors that are under the control of the organization.

- *External Issues:* Factors that the organization cannot control.

Let's look at a few examples of internal issues:

- *Organizational structure:* Defines the roles, responsibilities, accountability, and hierarchical positions in the organization. This helps define the position of the ISMS. Having clearly defined roles and responsibilities in securing the information helps you know who is responsible for which areas and provides clarity on what needs to be done.

- *Organizational culture:* The culture of the organization can be expressed in terms of the vision, mission, and values. The organizational policy, business strategies, and objectives also help define the information security policy. As per the standard ISO 27001:2013 Clause 5.2, organizations need to publish their information security policies. Considering employees perspectives is very important when publishing documents that will affect the way people work.

- *Available resources:* It is important to know which resources are available to the organization to implement information security. Knowing which technologies, systems, equipment, and personnel you already have helps guide you in terms of procurement or acquisition of resources.

Now let's look at some external issues. Here are a few examples:

- *Legal and regulatory requirements:* From an implementation point of view, it is essential to determine the legal, safety, and regulatory requirements of your organization. Some regulatory requirements— such as labor laws, IT-related safety requirements, and intellectual copyright law—are mandatory and must be met to be compliant. Chapter 6 covers the mandatory controls in detail.

- *Political and economic environment:* This also plays an important role when implementing ISMS, and you need to monitor government policy changes or changes in currency rate.

- *Technological trends:* New technologies may bring new security challenges and may require new ways to protect the information.

As seen in Figure 2-1, organizations need to determine their business context. For that, you need to identify the internal and external issues in your organization and identify the relevant interested parties.

Figure 2-1. *Interested parties and internal/external issues*

It is important to understand the business needs, which means you need to know the context of your business. In other words, why does your business exist? This will help you assess the business needs and strategize the ISO 27001 implementation.

Many organizations either skip or neglect to understand the business context. Then, during the scope planning, many areas are missed or unidentified and that can lead to problems because of incomplete scope analysis.

So, who should know or understand the business context? Every employee, contractor, and vendor who works with your organization should, because it directly or indirectly impacts the organization's business objectives. If the business context is not clear, workers won't be able to meet the organization's set objectives.

To understand this in a more holistic manner, let's look at this from different industry angles:

- *IT/hardware/software organization:* The company is doing software development work or providing IT services. Lots of customer data is handled by the company. If the solutions provided or the systems used by the company are not secure, it can impact company business and its reputation. Hence, it becomes important to secure business critical information in all possible ways.

- *Banking organization:* Banks handle your financial data and transactions and they must be protected from unauthorized access and theft. Their customers have put lot of faith in the bank and in its systems. If it gets breached, it can impact the bank's business and reputation. It's very important for bank to secure their systems and networks in all possible ways.

- *Healthcare organization:* These organizations handle and store patient healthcare information and it must be protected from unauthorized access and theft. Your customers won't be happy if their personal health information is made public or stolen. Victims could sue you, which in turn could impact the company's business and reputation. Hence, it's important for healthcare organizations to secure their systems and networks in all possible ways.

These are just a few examples to show you why it's worth it to invest your time and money in implementing ISO 27001 security practices.

Scope and High-level Timeframe for Implementation

Once you are clear about the business need, the next big step is to assess the scope of the implementation within the organization. It doesn't matter whether the organization is small, medium, or large.

Note   No matter how small or big the organization is, the scope assessment is very important, as it will provide an understanding to all stakeholders and employees including senior management, customers, and auditors about the areas in your organization that are part of the implementation.

There are numerous factors involved in identifying the scope. You need to consider the organization entities, locations, geographies, business units, departments, any products or services that are offered.

You need to look for areas that are out of scope from an implementation or certification point of view and then assess the impact on the overall implementation. For areas you find to be out of scope (not under your control or influence), you have to assess if important stakeholders or interested parties are affected.

So, how do you identify out of scope areas? You analyze business process flow and key dependencies between the activities performed by the organization and activities that are outsourced to another organization.

Say your organization has outsourced the hosting of datacenter services. The activities of the datacenter are out of your controlled scope, but you still need to manage your vendor as part of your outsourced policies and processes. They are responsible for managing your business and customer risks. You should also conduct a vendor risk assessment, which you will learn about in the coming chapters.

Tip   Look for vendors/suppliers who are compliant with information security practices, as this will help you feel confident that they understand your business risks.

By taking all these steps, you can rest easy that you have not missed any important areas or stakeholders.

You can take three main steps to identify the scope of implementation for your organization's ISMS:

1. Identify the areas/systems/locations where all the information is or will be stored. This includes the physical and digital document files.

2. Identify all the ways by which information is or will be made accessible to users.

3. Identify what is out of scope, i.e., what your organization doesn't have control over, such as outsourced products or services.

By taking these steps, you can prepare the following documents:

- Scope document

- Statement of applicability

A well-defined scope provides assurance that all the important areas of your organization have been covered in terms of implementing security controls. It also helps to get everyone, including management, on the same page, with one common vision. If this is not handled properly, it may delay or extend the implementation timeline. Documenting the organization's scope is one of the requirements of the ISO 27001 standard.

Many organizations have security departments, which are lead by the chief information security officer (CISO). This person usually reports directly to the vice president or managing director. The CISO has the authority to form a team to work on the implementation of ISO 27001. In general, the team includes the following members:

- *Steering committee members:* This includes the managing director, vice president, chief executive officer, chief technology officer, and the chief information security officer.

- *Information security department members:* This includes the information security manager, team members, and department heads of any departments that are part of the implementation. The information security department members schedule a meeting with the department heads to define their scope of work and determine what standard operating procedures they use on a daily basis to perform their tasks.

During such discussions, you can use a checklist or questionnaire to collect the information. This will help you conclude whether the collected information is important from a business point of view and can be placed under the crucial category. That is why this chapter discussed business context. You need to understand the business context in order to understand the systems and processes that you use in your organization.

Once all these department discussions are done, the team makes a collective decision to identify the overall scope of the organization, including the departments to be included, company locations, etc.

To decide on the final scope, a meeting is arranged with the steering committee members. The scope is presented to them and there might be multiple rounds of discussions. The CISO might need to explain the reasoning for selecting the identified scope, at which point it might be tweaked. There can be multiple rounds of this process.

Once management or the approval authority has approved everything, the scope can be frozen, and it becomes a guiding document for working on the implementation. The key is to manage the expectations of management.

Once the scope document is frozen, you might wonder whether it can be revised or modified. It can be revised based on the many inputs and scenarios observed during the implementation, because more clarity comes when you execute the tasks.

Team members must meet on a weekly basis to share information with the CISO, who can make initial decisions and determine whether the issues should be included in the scope. The final decision is the steering committee's as they know the budget requirements as well as the implementation requirements.

What's Covered in the Scope Document?

This section lists a sample table of contents for a scope document. It is for reference purposes only. This content may be modified or deleted based on the organization's requirements/knowledge/experience.

- *Purpose of the document*: Describe what is covered in the scope document.

- *Company/organization description*: A brief description of the organization, including the company's business.

- *Scope statement*: A statement that covers the primary objective of the ISMS implementation.

  - Within the scope: What is in the scope

  - Out of scope: Exclusions with justifications

  - Company stakeholders: Mention the key stakeholders

  - Company geographical/physical locations: Mention locations that are part of the implementation

  - Information security objectives: Mention the objectives to be achieved

  - Responsibilities of the information security group: Mention the key responsibilities in a clear manner

  - Monitoring and review: Mention the scenarios in which the scope document can be reviewed/revisited for any changes/additions

If you adequately cover all these points in your scope document, you will properly document your organization ISO 27001/ISMS implementation's scope. This can be shown to your customers or to auditors who need to know the scope and areas that are excluded.

What Is the Statement of Applicability (SOA)?

The Statement of Applicability (SOA) goes hand in hand with the scope identification exercise. It is an important document that helps you look for the areas to be included in your ISMS.

This document helps you select the controls that you implement within your organization. It is also a mandatory document and it's required to show the auditor or the certification body during the ISO 27001 certification exercise. It will act as a roadmap of your ISMS implementation and will ensure that your organization meets the standard criteria put forth by the international standard organization (ISO).

The sample SOA template explained in the following sections will help you understand the controls mentioned in the SOA. Then you can determine which controls are applicable to specific teams or members in your organization. When it is not clear which team member has the responsibility to implement certain controls, this document can help clarify the roles and responsibilities.

To provide more clarity and understanding, the following SOA tables have been provided with explanations. However, detailed explanations on how to do the implementations are covered in later chapters. See Tables 2-1 through 2-14.

Section A.5 of the Annexure

Table 2-1 shows Section A.5. This is the policy document that needs to be established based on the ISMS scope that's been finalized for the implementation.

Note   Security controls are categorized into *annexures* in the ISO 27001 standard.

Table 2-1. *A.5 Information Security Policies*

A.5	Information security policies	
A.5.1	Management direction for information security	
Objective: To provide management direction and support for information security in accordance with business requirements and relevant laws and regulations.		
A.5.1.1	Policies for information security	*Control* A set of policies for information security shall be defined, approved by management, published and communicated to employees and relevant external parties.
A.5.1.2	Review of the policies for information security	*Control* The policies for information security shall be reviewed at planned intervals or if significant changes occur to ensure their continuing suitability, adequacy and effectiveness.

Responsibility

The Information Security Department establishes the policy document after approval from management or another authority.

Section A.6 of the Annexure

As shown in Table 2-2, Section A.6 covers the controls that define the information security roles and responsibilities of each team member in the organization. Also, for each role, the duties must be segregated. This also secures teleworking equipment and portable devices.

Table 2-2. *A.6 Organization of Information Security*

A.6	Organization of information security	
A.6.1	**Internal organization**	
Objective: To establish a management framework to initiate and control the implementation and operation of information security within the organization.		
A.6.1.1	Information security roles and responsibilities	*Control* All information security responsibilities shall be defined and allocated.
A.6.1.2	Segregation of duties	*Control* Conflicting duties and areas of responsibility shall be segregated to reduce opportunities for unauthorized or unintentional modification or misuse of the organization's assets.
A.6.1.3	Contact with authorities	*Control* Appropriate contacts with relevant authorities shall be maintained.
A.6.1.4	Contact with special interest groups	*Control* Appropriate contacts with special interest groups or other specialist security forums and professional associations shall be maintained.
A.6.1.5	Information security in project management	*Control* Information security shall be addressed in project management, regardless of the type of the project.
A.6.2	**Mobile devices and teleworking**	
Objective: To ensure the security of teleworking and use of mobile devices.		
A.6.2.1	Mobile device policy	*Control* A policy and supporting security measures shall be adopted to manage the risks introduced by using mobile devices.
A.6.2.2	Teleworking	*Control* A policy and supporting security measures shall be implemented to protect information accessed, processed or stored at teleworking sites.

Responsibility

The Human Resources department should take the lead in establishing the roles and responsibilities of the team members. The Information Security department will act as a guide.

Section A.7 of the Annexure

As shown in Table 2-3, Section A.7 covers the controls to be implemented during the employee hiring process, from the point of being hired until termination or exit of the employee from the company.

Table 2-3. *A.7 Human Resource Security*

A.7	Human resource security	
A.7.1	**Prior to employment**	
Objective: To ensure that employees and contractors understand their responsibilities and are suitable for the roles for which they are considered.		
A.7.1.1	Screening	*Control* Background verification checks on all candidates for employment shall be carried out in accordance with relevant laws, regulations and ethics and shall be proportional to the business requirements, the classification of the information to be accessed and the perceived risks.
A.7.1.2	Terms and conditions of employment	*Control* The contractual agreements with employees and contractors shall state their and the organization's responsibilities for information security.
A.7.2	**During employment**	
Objective: To ensure that employees and contractors are aware of and fulfil their information security responsibilities.		
A.7.2.1	Management responsibilities	*Control* Management shall require all employees and contractors to apply information security in accordance with the established policies and procedures of the organization.
A.7.2.2	Information security awareness, education and training	*Control* All employees of the organization and, where relevant, contractors shall receive appropriate awareness education and training and regular updates in organizational policies and procedures, as relevant for their job function.
A.7.2.3	Disciplinary process	*Control* There shall be a formal and communicated disciplinary process in place to take action against employees who have committed an information security breach.
A.7.3	**Termination and change of employment**	
Objective: To protect the organization's interests as part of the process of changing or terminating employment.		
A.7.3.1	Termination or change of employment responsibilities	*Control* Information security responsibilities and duties that remain valid after termination or change of employment shall be defined, communicated to the employee or contractor and enforced.

Responsibility

All the controls should be owned by the Human Resources/recruitment team. The Information Security department will act as a guide.

Section A.8 of the Annexure

As shown in Table 2-4, Section A.8 covers the controls to be implemented to manage the information assets (could be hardware, software, people, information stored on paper, electronic media, etc.).

Table 2-4. *A.8 Asset Management*

A.8	Asset management	
A.8.1	**Responsibility for assets**	
Objective: To identify organizational assets and define appropriate protection responsibilities.		
A.8.1.1	Inventory of assets	*Control* Assets associated with information and information processing facilities shall be identified and an inventory of these assets shall be drawn up and maintained.
A.8.1.2	Ownership of assets	*Control* Assets maintained in the inventory shall be owned.
A.8.1.3	Acceptable use of assets	*Control* Rules for the acceptable use of information and of assets associated with information and information processing facilities shall be identified, documented and implemented.
A.8.1.4	Return of assets	*Control* All employees and external party users shall return all of the organizational assets in their possession upon termination of their employment, contract or agreement.

(*continued*)

Table 2-4. (*continued*)

A.8.2	Information classification	
Objective: To ensure that information receives an appropriate level of protection in accordance with its importance to the organization.		
A.8.2.1	Classification of information	*Control* Information shall be classified in terms of legal requirements, value, criticality and sensitivity to unauthorised disclosure or modification.
A.8.2.2	Labelling of information	*Control* An appropriate set of procedures for information labelling shall be developed and implemented in accordance with the information classification scheme adopted by the organization.
A.8.2.3	Handling of assets	*Control* Procedures for handling assets shall be developed and implemented in accordance with the information classification scheme adopted by the organization.
A.8.3	Media handling	
Objective: To prevent unauthorized disclosure, modification, removal or destruction of information stored on media.		
A.8.3.1	Management of removable media	*Control* Procedures shall be implemented for the management of removable media in accordance with the classification scheme adopted by the organization.
A.8.3.2	Disposal of media	*Control* Media shall be disposed of securely when no longer required, using formal procedures.
A.8.3.3	Physical media transfer	*Control* Media containing information shall be protected against unauthorized access, misuse or corruption during transportation.

Responsibility

Each department member is responsible for managing the assets produced or maintained by their department. The Information Security department will act as a guide.

Section A.9 of the Annexure

As shown in Table 2-5, Section A.9 covers the controls to be implemented to provide authorized access to the information and systems used to process the information.

Table 2-5. *A.9 Access Control*

A.9	Access control	
A.9.1	**Business requirements of access control**	
Objective:	To limit access to information and information processing facilities.	
A.9.1.1	Access control policy	*Control* An access control policy shall be established, documented and reviewed based on business and information security requirements.
A.9.1.2	Access to networks and network services	*Control* Users shall only be provided with access to the network and network services that they have been specifically authorized to use.
A.9.2	**User access management**	
Objective: To ensure authorized user access and to prevent unauthorized access to systems and services.		
A.9.2.1	User registration and de-registration	*Control* A formal user registration and de-registration process shall be implemented to enable assignment of access rights.
A.9.2.2	User access provisioning	*Control* A formal user access provisioning process shall be implemented to assign or revoke access rights for all user types to all systems and services.
A.9.2.3	Management of privileged access rights	*Control* The allocation and use of privileged access rights shall be restricted and controlled.
A.9.2.4	Management of secret authentication information of users	*Control* The allocation of secret authentication information shall be controlled through a formal management process.
A.9.2.5	Review of user access rights	*Control* Asset owners shall review users' access rights at regular intervals.
A.9.2.6	Removal or adjustment of access rights	*Control* The access rights of all employees and external party users to information and information processing facilities shall be removed upon termination of their employment, contract or agreement, or adjusted upon change.
A.9.3	**User responsibilities**	
Objective: To make users accountable for safeguarding their authentication information.		
A.9.3.1	Use of secret authentication information	*Control* Users shall be required to follow the organization's practices in the use of secret authentication information.
A.9.4	**System and application access control**	
Objective: To prevent unauthorized access to systems and applications.		
A.9.4.1	Information access restriction	*Control* Access to information and application system functions shall be restricted in accordance with the access control policy.
A.9.4.2	Secure log-on procedures	*Control* Where required by the access control policy, access to systems and applications shall be controlled by a secure log-on procedure.
A.9.4.3	Password management system	*Control* Password management systems shall be interactive and shall ensure quality passwords.
A.9.4.4	Use of privileged utility programs	*Control* The use of utility programs that might be capable of overriding system and application controls shall be restricted and tightly controlled.
A.9.4.5	Access control to program source code	*Control* Access to program source code shall be restricted.

Responsibility

The IT team is responsible for providing and monitoring the access to the organization's information. The Information Security department will act as a guide to all departments involved.

Section A.10 of the Annexure

As shown in Table 2-6, Section A.10 covers the controls to be implemented for cryptography, in order to secure the information.

Table 2-6. *A.10 Cryptography*

A.10	Cryptography	
A.10.1 Cryptographic controls		
Objective: To ensure proper and effective use of cryptography to protect the confidentiality, authenticity and/or integrity of information.		
A.10.1.1	Policy on the use of cryptographic controls	*Control* A policy on the use of cryptographic controls for protection of information shall be developed and implemented.
A.10.1.2	Key management	*Control* A policy on the use, protection and lifetime of cryptographic keys shall be developed and implemented through their whole lifecycle.

Responsibility

The IT team is responsible for implementing cryptographic controls over the information that's processed and stored on the systems.

Section A.11 of the Annexure

As shown in Table 2-7, Section A.11 covers the controls to be implemented to control access and permissions within the physical environmental workspace or office.

Table 2-7. *A.11 Physical and Environmental Security*

A.11.1 Secure areas		
Objective: To prevent unauthorized physical access, damage and interference to the organization's information and information processing facilities.		
A.11.1.1	Physical security perimeter	*Control* Security perimeters shall be defined and used to protect areas that contain either sensitive or critical information and information processing facilities.
A.11.1.2	Physical entry controls	*Control* Secure areas shall be protected by appropriate entry controls to ensure that only authorized personnel are allowed access.
A.11.1.3	Securing offices, rooms and facilities	*Control* Physical security for offices, rooms and facilities shall be designed and applied.
A.11.1.4	Protecting against external and environmental threats	*Control* Physical protection against natural disasters, malicious attack or accidents shall be designed and applied.
A.11.1.5	Working in secure areas	*Control* Procedures for working in secure areas shall be designed and applied.
A.11.1.6	Delivery and loading areas	*Control* Access points such as delivery and loading areas and other points where unauthorized persons could enter the premises shall be controlled and, if possible, isolated from information processing facilities to avoid unauthorized access.
A.11.2 Equipment		
Objective: To prevent loss, damage, theft or compromise of assets and interruption to the organization's operations.		
A.11.2.1	Equipment siting and protection	*Control* Equipment shall be sited and protected to reduce the risks from environmental threats and hazards, and opportunities for unauthorized access.
A.11.2.2	Supporting utilities	*Control* Equipment shall be protected from power failures and other disruptions caused by failures in supporting utilities.
A.11.2.3	Cabling security	*Control* Power and telecommunications cabling carrying data or supporting information services shall be protected from interception, interference or damage.
A.11.2.4	Equipment maintenance	*Control* Equipment shall be correctly maintained to ensure its continued availability and integrity.
A.11.2.5	Removal of assets	*Control* Equipment, information or software shall not be taken off-site without prior authorization.
A.11.2.6	Security of equipment and assets off-premises	*Control* Security shall be applied to off-site assets taking into account the different risks of working outside the organization's premises.
A.11.2.7	Secure disposal or re-use of equipment	*Control* All items of equipment containing storage media shall be verified to ensure that any sensitive data and licensed software has been removed or securely overwritten prior to disposal or re-use.
A.11.2.8	Unattended user equipment	*Control* Users shall ensure that unattended equipment has appropriate protection.
A.11.2.9	Clear desk and clear screen policy	*Control* A clear desk policy for papers and removable storage media and a clear screen policy for information processing facilities shall be adopted.

Responsibility

The IT and facility team is responsible for implementing the physical entry controls to your office locations and for securing the areas within your office.

Section A.12 of the Annexure

As shown in Table 2-8, Section A.12 covers the controls to be implemented for running smooth day-to-day operations in your organization.

Table 2-8. *A.12 Operation Security*

A.12	Operations security	
A.12.1 Operational procedures and responsibilities		
Objective: To ensure correct and secure operations of information processing facilities.		
A.12.1.1	Documented operating procedures	*Control* Operating procedures shall be documented and made available to all users who need them.
A.12.1.2	Change management	*Control* Changes to the organization, business processes, information processing facilities and systems that affect information security shall be controlled.
A.12.1.3	Capacity management	*Control* The use of resources shall be monitored, tuned and projections made of future capacity requirements to ensure the required system performance.
A.12.1.4	Separation of development, testing and operational environments	*Control* Development, testing, and operational environments shall be separated to reduce the risks of unauthorized access or changes to the operational environment.
A.12.2 Protection from malware		
Objective: To ensure that information and information processing facilities are protected against malware.		
A.12.2.1	Controls against malware	*Control* Detection, prevention and recovery controls to protect against malware shall be implemented, combined with appropriate user awareness.
A.12.3 Backup		
Objective: To protect against loss of data.		
A.12.3.1	Information backup	*Control* Backup copies of information, software and system images shall be taken and tested regularly in accordance with an agreed backup policy.

(*continued*)

Table 2-8. (*continued*)

A.12.4 Logging and monitoring		
Objective: To record events and generate evidence.		
A.12.4.1	Event logging	*Control* Event logs recording user activities, exceptions, faults and information security events shall be produced, kept and regularly reviewed.
A.12.4.2	Protection of log information	*Control* Logging facilities and log information shall be protected against tampering and unauthorized access.
A.12.4.3	Administrator and operator logs	*Control* System administrator and system operator activities shall be logged and the logs protected and regularly reviewed.
A.12.4.4	Clock synchronisation	*Control* The clocks of all relevant information processing systems within an organization or security domain shall be synchronised to a single reference time source.
A.12.5 Control of operational software		
Objective: To ensure the integrity of operational systems.		
A.12.5.1	Installation of software on operational systems	*Control* Procedures shall be implemented to control the installation of software on operational systems.
A.12.6 Technical vulnerability management		
Objective: To prevent exploitation of technical vulnerabilities.		
A.12.6.1	Management of technical vulnerabilities	*Control* Information about technical vulnerabilities of information systems being used shall be obtained in a timely fashion, the organization's exposure to such vulnerabilities evaluated and appropriate measures taken to address the associated risk.
A.12.6.2	Restrictions on software installation	*Control* Rules governing the installation of software by users shall be established and implemented.
A.12.7 Information systems audit considerations		
Objective: To minimise the impact of audit activities on operational systems.		
A.12.7.1	Information systems audit controls	*Control* Audit requirements and activities involving verification of operational systems shall be carefully planned and agreed to minimise disruptions to business processes.

Responsibility

The IT and facility teams are responsible for implementing operational controls.

Section A.13 of the Annexure

As shown in Table 2-9, Section A.13 covers the communication controls for securing the company's networks and the transfer of information from systems within and outside the organization.

Table 2-9. *A.13 Communication Security*

A.13	Communications security	
A.13.1 Network security management		
Objective: To ensure the protection of information in networks and its supporting information processing facilities.		
A.13.1.1	Network controls	*Control* Networks shall be managed and controlled to protect information in systems and applications.
A.13.1.2	Security of network services	*Control* Security mechanisms, service levels and management requirements of all network services shall be identified and included in network services agreements, whether these services are provided in-house or outsourced.
A.13.1.3	Segregation in networks	*Control* Groups of information services, users and information systems shall be segregated on networks.
A.13.2 Information transfer		
Objective: To maintain the security of information transferred within an organization and with any external entity.		
A.13.2.1	Information transfer policies and procedures	*Control* Formal transfer policies, procedures and controls shall be in place to protect the transfer of information through the use of all types of communication facilities.
A.13.2.2	Agreements on information transfer	*Control* Agreements shall address the secure transfer of business information between the organization and external parties.
A.13.2.3	Electronic messaging	*Control* Information involved in electronic messaging shall be appropriately protected.

Responsibility

The IT team is responsible for implementing controls on networks and on the transfer of information.

Section A.14 of the Annexure

As shown in Table 2-10, Section A.14 covers the controls to be followed during the development, testing, maintenance phases of your products and services.

Table 2-10. *A.14 System Acquisition Development and Maintenance*

A.14	System acquisition, development and maintenance	
A.14.1 Security requirements of information systems		
Objective: To ensure that information security is an integral part of information systems across the entire lifecycle. This also includes the requirements for information systems which provide services over public networks.		
A.14.1.1	Information security requirements analysis and specification	*Control* The information security related requirements shall be included in the requirements for new information systems or enhancements to existing information systems.
A.14.1.2	Securing application services on public networks	*Control* Information involved in application services passing over public networks shall be protected from fraudulent activity, contract dispute and unauthorized disclosure and modification.
A.14.1.3	Protecting application services transactions	*Control* Information involved in application service transactions shall be protected to prevent incomplete transmission, mis-routing, unauthorized message alteration, unauthorized disclosure, unauthorized message duplication or replay.

(*continued*)

Table 2-10. (*continued*)

A.14.2 Security in development and support processes		
Objective: To ensure that information security is designed and implemented within the development lifecycle of information systems.		
A.14.2.1	Secure development policy	*Control* Rules for the development of software and systems shall be established and applied to developments within the organization.
A.14.2.2	System change control procedures	*Control* Changes to systems within the development lifecycle shall be controlled by the use of formal change control procedures.
A.14.2.3	Technical review of applications after operating platform changes	*Control* When operating platforms are changed, business critical applications shall be reviewed and tested to ensure there is no adverse impact on organizational operations or security.
A.14.2.4	Restrictions on changes to software packages	*Control* Modifications to software packages shall be discouraged, limited to necessary changes and all changes shall be strictly controlled.
A.14.2.5	Secure system engineering principles	*Control* Principles for engineering secure systems shall be established, documented, maintained and applied to any information system implementation efforts.
A.14.2.6	Secure development environment	*Control* Organizations shall establish and appropriately protect secure development environments for system development and integration efforts that cover the entire system development lifecycle.
A.14.2.7	Outsourced development	*Control* The organization shall supervise and monitor the activity of outsourced system development.
A.14.2.8	System security testing	*Control* Testing of security functionality shall be carried out during development.
A.14.2.9	System acceptance testing	*Control* Acceptance testing programs and related criteria shall be established for new information systems, upgrades and new versions.
A.14.3 Test data		
Objective: To ensure the protection of data used for testing.		
A.14.3.1	Protection of test data	*Control* Test data shall be selected carefully, protected and controlled.

Responsibility

The IT team is responsible for implementing these controls. The Information Security team will act as a guide.

Section A.15 of the Annexure

As shown in Table 2-11, Section A.15 covers the controls to be followed during the procurement process of your products and services.

Table 2-11. *A.15 Supplier Relationships*

A.15	Supplier relationships	
A.15.1 Information security in supplier relationships		
Objective: To ensure protection of the organization's assets that is accessible by suppliers.		
A.15.1.1	Information security policy for supplier relationships	*Control* Information security requirements for mitigating the risks associated with supplier's access to the organization's assets shall be agreed with the supplier and documented.
A.15.1.2	Addressing security within supplier agreements	*Control* All relevant information security requirements shall be established and agreed with each supplier that may access, process, store, communicate, or provide IT infrastructure components for, the organization's information.
A.15.1.3	Information and communication technology supply chain	*Control* Agreements with suppliers shall include requirements to address the information security risks associated with information and communications technology services and product supply chain.
A.15.2 Supplier service delivery management		
Objective: To maintain an agreed level of information security and service delivery in line with supplier agreements.		
A.15.2.1	Monitoring and review of supplier services	*Control* Organizations shall regularly monitor, review and audit supplier service delivery.
A.15.2.2	Managing changes to supplier services	*Control* Changes to the provision of services by suppliers, including maintaining and improving existing information security policies, procedures and controls, shall be managed, taking account of the criticality of business information, systems and processes involved and re-assessment of risks.

Responsibility

The procurement and development team is responsible for implementing controls during the procurement process. This includes the procurement and product development team. The Information Security team will act as a guide.

Section A.16 of the Annexure

As shown in Table 2-12, Section A.16 covers the controls to be followed for all the incidents related to security, including communicating about security events and weaknesses.

Table 2-12. *A.16 Information Security Incident Management*

A.16	Information security incident management	
A.16.1 Management of information security incidents and improvements		
Objective: To ensure a consistent and effective approach to the management of information security incidents, including communication on security events and weaknesses.		
A.16.1.1	Responsibilities and procedures	*Control* Management responsibilities and procedures shall be established to ensure a quick, effective and orderly response to information security incidents.
A.16.1.2	Reporting information security events	*Control* Information security events shall be reported through appropriate management channels as quickly as possible.
A.16.1.3	Reporting information security weaknesses	*Control* Employees and contractors using the organization's information systems and services shall be required to note and report any observed or suspected information security weaknesses in systems or services.
A.16.1.4	Assessment of and decision on information security events	*Control* Information security events shall be assessed and it shall be decided if they are to be classified as information security incidents.
A.16.1.5	Response to information security incidents	*Control* Information security incidents shall be responded to in accordance with the documented procedures.
A.16.1.6	Learning from information security incidents	*Control* Knowledge gained from analysing and resolving information security incidents shall be used to reduce the likelihood or impact of future incidents.
A.16.1.7	Collection of evidence	*Control* The organization shall define and apply procedures for the identification, collection, acquisition and preservation of information, which can serve as evidence.

Responsibility

The IT department and all department stakeholders are responsible for implementing controls. Incidents can occur in any department and the department should note the incident. The Information Security team will act as a guide.

Section A.17 of the Annexure

As shown in Table 2-13, Section A.17 covers the controls required for business continuity.

Table 2-13. *A.17 Information Security Aspects of Business Continuity Management*

A.17	Information security aspects of business continuity management	
A.17.1	**Information security continuity**	
Objective: Information security continuity shall be embedded in the organization's business continuity management systems.		
A.17.1.1	Planning information security continuity	*Control* The organization shall determine its requirements for information security and the continuity of information security management in adverse situations, e.g. during a crisis or disaster.
A.17.1.2	Implementing information security continuity	*Control* The organization shall establish, document, implement and maintain processes, procedures and controls to ensure the required level of continuity for information security during an adverse situation.
A.17.1.3	Verify, review and evaluate information security continuity	*Control* The organization shall verify the established and implemented information security continuity controls at regular intervals in order to ensure that they are valid and effective during adverse situations.
A.17.2	**Redundancies**	
Objective: To ensure availability of information processing facilities.		
A.17.2.1	Availability of information processing facilities	*Control* Information processing facilities shall be implemented with redundancy sufficient to meet availability requirements.

Responsibility

The IT department and all accountable stakeholders will be responsible for implementing these controls. Business continuity allows the business to run smoothly during incidents that are not in the company's control. The Information Security team will act as a guide.

Section A.18 of the Annexure

As shown in Table 2-14, Section A.18 covers the controls required to maintain compliance with respect to all the controls mentioned in SOA.

Table 2-14. *A.18 Compliance*

A.18	Compliance	
A.18.1 Compliance with legal and contractual requirements		
Objective: To avoid breaches of legal, statutory, regulatory or contractual obligations related to information security and of any security requirements.		
A.18.1.1	Identification of applicable legislation and contractual requirements	*Control* All relevant legislative statutory, regulatory, contractual requirements and the organization's approach to meet these requirements shall be explicitly identified, documented and kept up to date for each information system and the organization.
A.18.1.2	Intellectual property rights	*Control* Appropriate procedures shall be implemented to ensure compliance with legislative, regulatory and contractual requirements related to intellectual property rights and use of proprietary software products.
A.18.1.3	Protection of records	*Control* Records shall be protected from loss, destruction, falsification, unauthorized access and unauthorized release, in accordance with legislatory, regulatory, contractual and business requirements.
A.18.1.4	Privacy and protection of personally identifiable information	*Control* Privacy and protection of personally identifiable information shall be ensured as required in relevant legislation and regulation where applicable.
A.18.1.5	Regulation of cryptographic controls	*Control* Cryptographic controls shall be used in compliance with all relevant agreements, legislation and regulations.
A.18.2 Information security reviews		
Objective: To ensure that information security is implemented and operated in accordance with the organizational policies and procedures.		
A.18.2.1	Independent review of information security	*Control* The organization's approach to managing information security and its implementation (i.e. control objectives, controls, policies, processes and procedures for information security) shall be reviewed independently at planned intervals or when significant changes occur.
A.18.2.2	Compliance with security policies and standards	*Control* Managers shall regularly review the compliance of information processing and procedures within their area of responsibility with the appropriate security policies, standards and any other security requirements.
A.18.2.3	Technical compliance review	*Control* Information systems shall be regularly reviewed for compliance with the organization's information security policies and standards.

Responsibility

The information Security team is responsible for checking and maintaining compliance with respect to all applicable controls. The Information Security team will act as a guide.

High-Level Timeframe

Once the ISMS scope is defined and you have a clear understanding of what is needed to implement it, you need to create a timeframe to achieve the objectives.

We all know that an ounce of prevention is better than a pound of cure. That means it's better to implement all needed security controls to prevent security incidents rather than have to address and fix incidents as they happen.

It is always tricky to determine the timeframe for implementation, as there are many dependencies and constraints for teams who will be working on this project. Sometimes, the timeline may come directly from management as a mandate to finish by a certain deadline. In that case, it becomes a top priority for various teams involved to work and deliver in a timely manner.

Consider these real-life examples of dependencies and constraints:

- *Commitment from the management and employees:* If you don't have commitment from the top, your project will not get support from the various stakeholders. You'll read more about the importance of management's commitment in the next section.

- *Budget issues and tool availability:* In order to implement security controls, you need many software tools that will help you ensure you achieve and maintain the compliance levels. If you're waiting for budget approvals and tools, your implementation timeline needs to be defined accordingly.

- *Current compliance/gap levels:* This will help you determine where you stand today in terms of your compliance levels and where you want to end up. If the majority of the security controls have not been implemented at the time of timeframe planning, a very clear input and timeframe should be carefully planned.

- *Geographies/locations:* This will help you determine which areas of the organization will be covered. Organizations usually prefer to implement the ISMS at all company locations simultaneously, but this depends on how big the implementation team is and the commitment level of management to provide the time and resources. If the implementation team is small and the work has been planned in a phase-wise manner, ask management for guidance as to which entity should be implemented first.

These scenarios may help you identify the areas, dependencies, and constraints that could impact your implementation's timeframe. It is important to create a realistic and achievable timeframe. Otherwise, you may feel unnecessary pressure to implement features in a shorter timeframe, which could impact the quality of security controls and the desired result.

The next chapter looks at the example of a *high-level timeframe,* which might help you identify the tasks involved and the timeline needed to complete the implementation.

Senior Management Support

You can increase the chances of having a successful implementation by bringing in top management. Without the support of management, your project will probably fail. Hence senior management support is essential. By support, it means that they are willing to provide all the resources required to implement information security. This could be human resources or the money required to support the project.

You need management support because the ISMS implementation process will be done by the departments and their team members. Top management may need to outline and define their expected roles, based on the overall priorities of the company, especially when these conflict with that group's or project's short-term priorities.

To get top management support, the CISO (Chief Information Security Information) or the person with the authority needs to present the ISMS/ISO 27001 project as a business case to senior management. They need to communicate the tangible and intangible benefits of the implementation.

You can increase the chances of a successful ISMS/ISO 27001 implementation by getting management buy-in. Without the support of management, the ISMS implementation might fail or may not lead to the desired result. Many security controls come with a cost and you will probably need top-level support to okay those costs.

Senior management should be willing to provide all the resources required to implement ISMS/ISO 27001 information security. Resources could be human, tools, budget, etc.

Top management's commitment and involvement can make the expected benefits of the ISMS program achievable, as follows:

- Meet the organization's strategic objectives

- Create a risk-management program to effectively manage risks

- Manage resources efficiently

- Create value-added initiatives

Note   Clause 5.1 emphasizes top management commitment.

Summary

In this chapter, you learned about the importance of the first step in implementation, which is to assess and understand the business needs and the context of the organization. You also learned how to finalize the scope of the implementation by creating a roadmap for ISMS/ISO 27001 implementation. You read about the important things to keep in mind when deciding the timeframe. You also learned that it's critical to get full support from management, in order to make your implementation achievable and useful.

Reference

https://www.iso.org/isoiec-27001-information-security.html

CHAPTER 3

Project Kick-Off

If I had six hours to chop down a tree, I'd spend the first four hours sharpening the axe.

—Abraham Lincoln

In the previous chapter, you learned about setting the scope and timeline of your implementation. It then becomes essential to kick off the ISMS implementation project in your organization, as it will help communicate to all key stakeholders/interested parties/employees that information security practices will be implemented and rolled out throughout the organization. It is the duty of every employee to adhere to these policies and all departments need to provide support in making the implementation successful.

When you formally start a project, the kick-off is an important activity to have with project stakeholders. This chapter explains how to conduct the ISO 27001 implementation kick-off with stakeholders. This chapter also talks about how to get stakeholder and team commitment on the project and how to set the timeline and create the project taskforce.

This chapter covers:

- Presenting the high-level plan

- Setting up the project taskforce

- Getting commitment from stakeholdets

We started this chapter with the famous quote by Abraham Lincoln, "If I had six hours to chop down a tree, I'd spend the first four hours sharpening the axe".

This means you should spend most of your time preparing for a task. Planning is an important step when working on ISO 27001 implementation projects.

© Abhishek Chopra, Mukund Chaudhary 2020
A. Chopra and M. Chaudhary, *Implementing an Information Security Management System*,
https://doi.org/10.1007/978-1-4842-5413-4_3

Presenting a High-Level Plan

When you're implementing a high-level plan, it is advisable to invite all the stakeholders and to set up high-level policies for information security. This involves:

- Setting up roles and responsibilities

- Defining rules for continual improvement

- Raising awareness of the team by providing them with regular training and communication

So, how do you initiate a kick-off? The CISO (Chief Information Security Officer) or relevant authoritative person must organize the kick-off meeting and invite all the key stakeholders associated with or working with the information security department. Many times, stakeholders are not aware of their role in the implementation, as the kick-off meeting is never planned. Hence, a project's importance fades over time and the expected result becomes difficult to achieve or the timeline gets extended.

Once all the key stakeholders are present, it is very important to clearly communicate expectations. During the kick-off, you should also get lots of input, such as risks/issues/constraints that you'll need to overcome during implementation. The information security implementation team must track and resolve these issues as soon as possible.

Tip   It's critical that all stakeholders agree to the timeline, as they must provide the time to the project team, apart from their day-to-day tasks.

Figure 3-1 shows a high-level timeframe example. It should give you an overall idea about the tasks and activities that need to be completed and implemented.

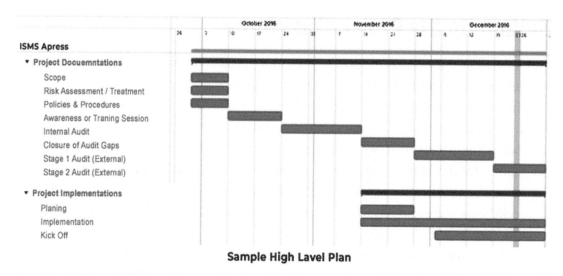

Sample High Lavel Plan

Figure 3-1. *High-level timelines*

Here are example activities that are covered when implementing ISMS:

- Scope

- Risk assessment

- Risk treatment

- Defining policies and procedures

- Awareness or training sessions

- Controls implementation

- Internal audit

- Closure of audit gaps

- Stage 1 audit (external)

- Stage 2 audit (external)

This is not an exhaustive list; there may be other activities, depending on your organization. The duration of each task could vary from one organization to another, as the required skills and scope of work may be different. Hence, the organization/implementation teams must keep in mind these factors before getting commitment from the stakeholders.

Setting Up the Project Taskforce

We all know that without team members' support, projects aren't successful. Hence, it is very important to set up the taskforce in order to implement the ISO 27001.

The project team can be selected based on the scope of the ISMS. For example, if you are implementing ISO 27001 in multiple locations of your organization, the scope is big and the same team does not work at all locations. It would be better to select teams geographically, in terms of where the actual implementation and audit will happen. Similarly, if you are implementing the ISMS in a single location and the scope is limited to one division/branch of your organization, the scope will be small and the team size will also vary.

Having said that, the taskforce setup depends on the scope of the ISMS, the resource availability of the organization, and the skill of the people. There is no fixed requirement from the standard to have certain people with certain roles implement the ISMS. It is good to have some key people supervise the implementation along with the management team.

Setting up the taskforce early in the planning and implementation stages will lead to better success. The team can take part in the kick-off meetings, which will make them confident as a team and give them the chance to get to know each other better.

Administration Department

The administration department can be represented as a SPOC (single point of contact) for managing and implementing the physical, operational, and facility related aspects of the ISMS framework. They can enable the acknowledgment of guidelines, procedures, and policies inside the organization in adherence with the ISO 27001 requirements. The authority and responsibility of the role can be defined by the organization.

Chief Information Security Officer (CISO)

The Chief Information Security Officer is primarily responsible for preparing, maintaining, and communicating the information security policies and procedures within the organization.

This person is considered the administrative head of security. The CISO is responsible for security awareness and serves as a focal point for deciding all security issues. Some key responsibilities of the CISO are to:

- Lead the information security initiative and the information-security related activities.

- Prepare security guidelines for the information security management team.

- Maintain the ISMS, establish the security risk assessment process, and review the risk assessment reports and status. The next chapter discusses these terms in detail.

- Maintain the statement of applicability.

- Monitor ongoing compliance with security standards in the organization.

- Prepare management and information related plans and procedures.

- Ensure that the team members are adequately trained on the physical security domain in order to meet the security requirements of ISO 27001.

- Analyze the reports prepared by various support departments and take corrective action when required.

- Plan and conduct information security internal audits and management reviews.

- Ensure that corrective actions are taken against the issues raised during the internal or external audits.

- Report on the performance of the ISMS to top management.

System Admin or IT Manager

This is one of the most important roles in the ISMS implementation. This person is responsible for maintaining the security of the organization's network and other information-processing facilities. This includes ensuring that all network resources are protected from unauthorized access, initiating corrective measures, and reporting security breaches or incidents. Some of the key responsibilities expected from this role include, but are not limited to:

- Implement the logical security measures over networking systems and ensure all networking resources are protected from unauthorized access.

- Assess vulnerabilities in the present networking system and monitor firewall and router security.

- Review network logs and incidents to ensure the security of network OS.

- Escalate any illegal activities to senior management and to the information security management team immediately.

- Evaluate and recommend new security products be implemented across the organization and report their utility and benefits to the organization.

Information Security Management (ISM) Team

This team may have members from each department or function included in the information security scope. The ISM team is primarily responsible for incident reporting and response. The team may also participate in internal auditing and business continuity/disaster recovery.

Human Resources Management

The human resources team is responsible managing and enabling the acknowledgment of HR guidelines, procedures, and policies inside the organization in adherence with ISO 27001 requirements. Some of the key responsibilities of the HR team include:

- Follow and comply with the HR requirements as dictated by the ISO 27001 framework.

- Release the documents of ISO 27001 to appropriate personnel inside the organization.

- Establish the HR department as the SPOC for ISO 27001 between the employees and the management.

- Ensure that training, development, and background verifications/ referral checks are completed on all employees.

These roles may entail more or less responsibility depending on the organization you are working in and the nature of the business. The team can be expanded or modified as per the organization's need.

Note   The titles of these roles may be different, and the titles illustrated in this book are for understanding purposes only. They might be similar or completely different and they depend on the organization's needs and the nature of their business.

Getting Commitment

This important step involves getting commitment from the team. After conducting a kick-off and presenting the high-level plan to all the stakeholders, it's important to get commitment from all affected parties.

Commitment to achieve something new mostly comes from the top. Once you get management-level commitment, it's easier to get commitment from the people doing the work. As an example, say you have one highly skilled resource in your organization, Henry, who you think can help with the ISO 27001 implementation. Henry is actively involved with another project and reports to a different manager. In this case, if you approach him without the proper management approval, chances are he will not work with you, as he has other priorities.

In order to get Henry to work on your project, you need to get approval from his manager. Of course, individual team member commitment also depends on whether management is committed to the ISMS project.

To get the commitment and support of team members, it is best to have clearly defined roles and responsibilities for every team member and these must be approved by top management.

If the management team is not supportive or involved—if they are not interested and don't participate in management reviews—then your initiatives are not likely to succeed.

During the ISO 27001 audit, management commitment is checked for compliance to the standard. If the auditor observes during the audit that management commitment is weak, he might assume that implementation is also weak.

Such a scenario may not go well with the auditor's team members. The auditor might feel that the teams will not get the management support they need to implement the standard requirements in an effective manner.

A poor audit can be a showstopper from the organization and team's point of view. After all, auditors don't come in every day to do audits and share their experiences. If the company is implementing the standard for the first time, it becomes very important to learn and implement best practices.

Thus, management commitment is the driving force of each step you are taking to implement the ISMS or ISO 27001 standard. Other stakeholders/members you would expect commitment from are those who are either involved in the decision-making process or are implementers.

Decision makers and implementers will spend most of their time implementing the ISMS. Hence, getting their commitment is very important. It is also very important to have a balance of commitment levels from management and the other stakeholders. If this is mismatched, it will impact the implementation and the overall results.

To manage these scenarios, the ISO 27001 standard includes Clause 5.3, Organizational Roles, Responsibilities, and Authorities, which states that "top management shall ensure that the responsibilities and authorities for roles relevant to information security are assigned and communicated".

Top management shall assign the responsibility and authority for:

- Ensuring that the information security management system conforms to the requirements of this international standard

- Reporting on the performance of the information security management system to top management

Source: ISO/IEC 27001 Standard Second Edition

Note   Top management may also assign responsibilities for reporting the performance of the information security management system within the organization.

Commitment to information security must be driven from the top to the bottom. It is also very important to have a balance of commitment levels from management and the other stakeholders.

Let's consider how you can get this commitment, by using the following example form. From this form, stakeholders can better understand the following key points:

- The ISO 27001 standard is a management framework and it focuses on risks catering to the processes of the organization.

- Security controls can be IT related but they are mostly business oriented. IT acts as a tool to implement security controls to meet the ISO 27001 requirements.

- ISO is not an IT certification. It is a business certification and it is the responsibility of everyone to control/protect the information.

- Risk management should be institutionalized as a practice throughout the organization. For this, the risk register has to be maintained.

- The organization must place business continuity controls to ensure the continuity of its business services.

- The organization must perform regular internal audits and plan/ conduct three-year cycle external audits.

- By signing the commitment form, every member acknowledges the effort required to implement the ISMS/ISO 27001.

The sample form has the following points:

- The management is committed to the requirements of the ISO 27001.

- Members are aware of the ISO 27001 initiative and have agreed to work with the implementation team toward a successful ISMS implementation.

- The management and staff commit to maintaining the security standards, even after the initial certification, to ensure continued compliance.

- The management and staff commit to continually improving the information security approach.

These points should be described on the commitment form that all affected parties sign, as shown in Figure 3-2.

ISO 27001 - Agreement Form / Signatures

| Project Name: | |
| CISO Name: | |

I have reviewed the information contained in this Project Commitments – Agreement Form *and agree:*

Name	Title	Signature	Date (MM/DD/YY)

The signatures above indicate an understanding of the purpose and content of this document by those signing it. By signing this document, they agree to this as the formal Project Commitments – Agreement Form.

Figure 3-2. *Sample commitment signature format*

Summary

This chapter talked about a high-level plan for implementing ISO 27001. It also touched on how to set up the project taskforce, which is required to execute the project. It briefly talked about their roles and responsibilities. You also learned about the importance of getting commitment from the team as well as from upper management in order to kick off the project.

The next chapter covers identifying risk related to information security. You'll learn about how to do risk assessment and report it to stakeholders.

CHAPTER 4

Initial Risk Assessment

Business people need to understand the psychology of risk more than the mathematics of risk.

—Paul Gibbons

The previous chapter emphasized the importance of the kick-off meeting with the implementation teams. This chapter focuses on meeting the team members to conduct the initial risk assessment.

This chapter lays the foundation for the initial risk identification and assessment and talks about the importance of preparing and presenting the findings report.

Meeting the Team

To plan the meeting or risk assessment sessions, first meet with the individual teams one by one. That way, you can focus on the areas that each team is responsible for, and it will reduce the chances of missing a key security area.

Meeting all the teams at the same time in a group might not be easy to handle because the security controls for each team may vary. Some have more or less compliance issues. Some teams might lose interest in the first meeting as they may feel their contribution is small. So be careful when implementing big projects.

Identified risks should be reviewed together with all the teams that are affected by those risks, in order to have better risk management plans. Although you can get the help of subject matter experts, it's better if the risk is identified by those people who are the process owners, as in ISMS/ISO 27001 implementation, the emphasis is more on your process steps, your information flow, or your storage.

© Abhishek Chopra, Mukund Chaudhary 2020
A. Chopra and M. Chaudhary, *Implementing an Information Security Management System,*
https://doi.org/10.1007/978-1-4842-5413-4_4

You might wonder which team to meet with first. This is a common question across different organizations, as information security teams must meet with many departments to conduct organization-level risk assessment exercises. Most of the time, information security team/CISO just sets up the team.

When most of the members are new to the team or if you are new to the organization, it's important that you involve someone who understands the business context of the company. In previous chapters, you learned about the importance of knowing the business context.

Hence, the information security team might hesitate when they need to analyze risk of large organizations or reach out to people who have presence in multiple locations. It becomes easier for teams that have some experience (a year minimum) and have started to implement some key security controls. They already know people or different teams and can start to know about the information security team, which will help to build rapport with other teams.

In some organizations, information security is an area that they are hearing about for the first time; they do not know what is expected from them. In that case, knowing people and building relationships will help to overcome the challenges.

Some departments aren't even aware that an information security department exists within their organization, which is a problem because they cannot work in isolation. Hence it is the responsibility of the information security department to meet all the relevant departments as soon as possible.

The next sections discuss how to analyze gaps with the different teams. In these cases, you are starting to determine the gaps using the control provided in the ISO/IEC 27001 standard.

Annex 5: Information Security Policies

Check whether the company has done the following:

- Defined information security policies.

- Communicated these policies to employees and other relevant stakeholders.

- Reviewed the policies at regular intervals.

During the assessment, you need to check the levels of implementation and assess what is missing.

Note   In most organizations, these steps aren't performed prior to the ISMS/ISO 27001 implementation.

Annex 6: Organization of Information Security

Check whether the company has done the following:

- Defined and allocated information security responsibilities.

- Clearly segregated duties. There should be no conflict of duties or areas of responsibility that overlap, creating dual roles.

- Defined procedures to maintain appropriate contacts with relevant authorities.

- Maintained contact with special interest groups for knowledge improvement purposes.

- Identified and addressed risks in information security during the project's lifecycle.

- Ensured proper mobile device use and safe telecommuting. Check how this policy has been defined and implemented.

During the assessment, you check the levels of implementation and assess what is missing.

Annex 7: Human Resources Security

Check whether the company has done the following:

- *Before employment*

  - Conduct employee background verification checks.

  - Look for any report prepared in reference to background checks.

  - Ensure that terms and conditions of employment are communicated properly to employees and contractors.

- *During employment*

  - Check how management responsibilities are implemented.

  - Ensure that employee/contractor education and training has been conducted and recorded.

  - Check how the disciplinary process is established and communicated to employees and contractors and whether any disciplinary action is taken once they have committed an information security breach.

- *Termination and change of employment*

  - Ensure that employee and contractor termination or change of employment practices are conducted and managed properly.

Annex 8: Asset Management

This control emphasizes how organizational assets are identified and what responsibilities are defined for the protection of assets. To identify the initial risk assessment from this control, you need to check the following things:

- Check how assets are identified and whether there is inventory throughout the asset lifecycle.

- Check how ownership of assets is defined and allotted to the asset owner.

- Check how acceptable usage policies are defined and communicated to all asset users.

- Check how employees and contractors return company assets upon their termination.

- Check how information classification is done for the various types of information generated in your organization to prevent its unintended disclosure.

- Check whether a procedure is defined to label information (electronic format) and any related physical assets.

- Check whether a procedure is defined for handling various types of assets.

- Ensure that media is removed properly when it is no longer required.

- Ensure that media is disposed of properly when it is no longer needed.

- Check how media is protected from unauthorized access, misuse, or corruption when transported out of the office.

Annex 9: Access Control

Access control is essential for all types of organizations. An access control policy should be established, documented, and controlled based on the organization's need. To identify the initial risk assessment, you need to check the following things:

- Check for the access control policies that segregate the access control roles. For example, access requests, access authorizations, and access administration.

- Check whether all important passwords and credentials are stored securely.

- Check that everyone in the organization has only role-based access and they can view or modify only what they are supposed to.

- Check that the access rights are associated with all the systems, tools, or software that employees use and have proper access management.

- Check the development environment and ensure that the source code is restricted to authorized users only.

Annex 10: Cryptographic Control

Do you still store or transport business confidential information in pen drives, hard drives, and other external drives? If the answer is yes, consider the potential impact of losing that data or it being stolen by a competitor. To avoid these scenarios, it's smart use cryptographic control.

Cryptography control ensures confidentiality, authenticity, and integrity of information. Consider these points to analyze the implementation gap in cryptographic controls:

- Does the organization have an encryption policy that defines the proper use of encryption tools and defines the strength and quality of encryption algorithm? The policy document should also address key management and define methods for dealing with protecting keys and information.

- Check how the keys are managed after their generation and how they are stored and distributed.

- Check for rules, regulations, and restrictions regarding the use of cryptographic controls in the country where you are implementing ISMS.

- Check that all your web applications are secured and configured with the latest TLS and SSL.

- Check how your payment information is encrypted during the transaction and how you store the payment information in your database.

By asking these questions, you can determine if any gaps exist regarding this control.

Annex 11: Physical and Environmental Security

This next control involves physical and environmental security. The main objective of this control is to keep the organization's workplace environment safe and secure. To identify the initial risk from this control, you need to identify the gaps in the following areas:

- Check that the office is well protected against unauthorized access and that all the doors and windows are properly locked during non-office/non-activity hours.

- Check that the security and fire alarms are configured and tested.

- Check that your company maintains visitor logs, with details like their time in, time out, purpose of meeting, etc.

- Check that all the employees have an access card to enter the premises and that highly sensitive zones like server rooms and other zones identified by your organization are also protected by biometrics.

- Check that the fire alarms, smoke detectors, water sprinklers, and fire extinguishers are installed and regularly tested. Also, check that the fire safety drill training has been conducted.

- Check that business-critical equipment is protected from unauthorized access.

- Check how the supporting utilities, such power supply, water, ventilation, and air conditioning are managed during an interruption.

- Check how the cabling security is managed to prevent damage.

- Check that all the supporting utilities or the equipment have undergone regular maintenance and that the records are maintained.

- Check how the removal of asset such as equipment, information, and software and its return to the organization is managed.

- Check for procedures or policies regarding when employees can work from home.

- Check how you manage transferring equipment from the office premises to external vendors.

- Check if you have a policy to dispose of or re-use equipment. Check whether you need third-party help or your organization can do it.

- Check how users' unattended equipment is protected and managed.

- Check if you have implemented a policy regarding clear desk and screens.

Note   All these points need to be checked thoroughly to identify initial risks, as there could be organizational obligations to implement them.

Annex 12: Operations Security

This control emphasizes the security of the day-to-day operations of the organization and the standard operating procedures (SOP) that are documented and made available to all employees to perform their daily work. To identify any initial risks, you need to check the following:

- Check that there are documented standard operating procedures so that teams know how to perform their daily work.

- Check how the change-management practices are implemented.

- Check how the capacity management practices (for applications, systems, databases, and environment) are planned and implemented.

- Check how you differentiate between environments (for development, testing, and production/live).

- Check what controls are implemented against malware detection, prevention, and recovery. Also, check for a policy that forbids the use of unauthorized software.

- Check that there is a policy that defines how to properly back up data.

- Check how the logs are maintained and reviewed for various events that occur during day-to-day operations.

- Check how the organization protects log information such as audit logs and various system logs.

- Check how the system administrator logs have been protected and reviewed regularly.

- Check how the clocks of all relevant information processing systems have been configured.

- Check that all installed operational software is licensed and check that they are installed, maintained, and upgraded on a regular basis.

- Check how your team conducts the vulnerability assessment test on your applications before they are released to production/live environment.

- Check which restrictions are implemented to prevent the installation of software packages without approval.

- Check that a policy has been implemented to perform an audit test on your day-to-day operations.

Annex 13: Communications Security

Communications security emphasizes the communication channel and the transfer of information by various means. The communication channel must be protected to secure your information.

To identify any initial risks from this control, you need to analyze the following:

- Check what control has been implemented to protect the company network for secure transfer of information.

- Check whether the network service providers are in-house or external to the organization. If they are external, check for the agreement and the service level agreed to protect the network.

- Check whether any network segregation levels are done.

- Check that information transfer practices have been implemented for transferring information within and outside the organization.

- Check which control has been implemented to protect information transfer via electronic messaging such as email, electronic data interchange, and social networking sites.

- Check how the non-disclosure agreement (NDA)/confidentiality agreement has been designed and implemented in your organization.

The next sections discuss analyzing the gaps in system acquisition, development, and maintenance.

Annex 14: Security Requirements of Information Systems

In any organization that has an IT department, this security control is applicable, as it emphasizes the security needed when building a software product or application.

The service delivery team makes up the program managers, project managers, business analysts, and QA managers. They are involved in the collection of products and applications during the requirement elicitation phase. They also communicate with the client or stakeholders daily. Hence, it is easier for them to understand what security requirements need to be built for the software.

The service delivery team is the right stakeholder to ask about this security requirement control. They have more clarity about whether this control is implemented per the standards, whether it is only partially implemented, or whether it's not implemented at all. Sometimes teams are not aware of which security requirements they need to collect as part of the requirement elicitation phase. Sometimes they are collecting a few, but they are not aware as what to collect as part of the security requirements. Because of this, the software applications could be easily hacked or compromised.

How and where do you collect security requirements? This is usually covered in the business requirement document or in the software requirement specification. They are sometimes referred to as BRS and SRS documents. Some organizations use software tools such as Jira Asana to store their product requirements. Hence, during the assessment of the security control, it is advised to go through the requirement descriptions to determine whether security requirements have been captured. This will help you assess the gaps in the current implementation.

Here are some examples of security requirements:

- *Level of access provided to the users.* For example, you need to show some sensitive information to an authorized customer or user after validating their authenticity. It can be a payment page which will appear only when the user is successfully logged in to the system. The user must be authorized and authenticated to the defined role to access the information.

- *Encryption of sensitive data.* For example, if you are collecting payment from the customer, the payment page must be encrypted so that the information transferred to the server will not leak or get hacked before reaching the payment gateway. If the information is leaked, it will not be of use to the hacker as it is encrypted. Another example is how you store customers' sensitive information such as credit card numbers and passwords. They also must be stored in encrypted format.

- *Session management.* Session management is mandatory for the stateless protocol HTTP as it authenticates the validity of authorization. The security requirement may be to see the inactivity of the user and close the session. In such a scenario, the user needs to log in again to validate authenticity.

There may be different security requirements based on the application or the software product you are working on. The standard makes it mandatory to collect those requirements and to comply with the regulations.

Security in Development and Support Processes

The objective of Clause 14.2 is to ensure that when the development team works, the development lifecycle will remain secure throughout the development or product's/application's life.

Define a Secure Development Policy

The secure development policy should guide the development team, and all must adhere to this security policy. The security policy should cover at least these issues (there could be others):

- Securing the coding environment, including the development environment and server, testing environment and server, and the production environment and server. As per the standard, these environments must be separate, and their access must always be protected and monitored.

- Secure coding guidelines. Developers should use secure coding methods when writing the code and commit fewer mistakes. This will help protect the code against virus and malware attacks. They need to install the latest security patches as well.

- Secure repositories, such as SVN, CVS, and GIT, by ensuring versions are maintained and controlled at all times. From time to time, developers must be trained in the secure coding practices.

- System change control. Changes must be incorporated using the change control procedures and with the approval of the change control board. The board should approve all changes. It is never safe to allow any one individual to decide to make such changes.

- Technical review. This refers to reviewing an application after any operating platform changes. This is to ensure that all business-critical applications have been reviewed/tested and are not compromised in any manner.

- Restriction of changes to software packages. It should not be allowed by the users on their own. It must be done by the IT members authorized to maintain all the software licenses. It is advisable to use the vendor supplied software packages. From time to time, the software should get updates and approved patches.

- Secure system engineering principles should be written according to your organization's in-house development activities. Security should be built at all levels and if any new technology or designs are added, they must be reviewed for security risks.

- Outsourced development. Whenever development needs to be outsourced, there are many controls to be placed. When we share code with other companies, it must be protected. The ownership of the code must be ensured and intellectual property rights must be respected.

- System security testing. There needs to be thorough testing of newly developed and updated systems. For in-house development, the development team should perform the testing first and then an independent testing team should test the product or the application.

- System acceptance testing must be done for all new systems or upgrades. Testing must be done in a real environment to ensure that the system does not have any security vulnerabilities.

Test Data

The objective of Clause 14.3 is to ensure that the test data is selected carefully, protected, and controlled.

The main point is to remember while performing testing, is to avoid personal identifiable information and confidential information. Once the testing is done, all data must be immediately erased from all the testing environments.

Annex 15: Supplier Relationships

Supplier relationships need to protect the business information that is shared between the suppliers. To identify the initial risk associated with this control, you need to ask the following questions:

- Check whether signed non-disclosure agreements are available from all vendors and suppliers.

- Check how security parameters (such as legal and regulatory requirements, intellectual property rights, and copyright) are covered in the agreement signed with your suppliers/vendors.

- Check how the supplier agreements about supply chain security and appropriate security practices throughout the supply chain have been implemented.

- Check whether your organization is regularly monitoring, reviewing, and auditing the supplier service delivery for the services procured or outsourced.

- Check how changes to the supplier services are managed.

Annex 16: Information Security Incident Management

This control will help you effectively manage security incidents within your organization. Consider the following points while doing the initial risk assessment.

- Check whether any roles and responsibilities are defined that manage security incidents.

- Check how information security incidents are reported in the organization.

- Check how suspected weakness are observed and reported in the organization by responsible departments and by suppliers or vendors.

- Check how information security incidents are identified and reported to the information security incident reporting team (ISIRT).

- Check how the information security incidents are responded to and documented.

- Check whether your organization has a knowledgebase to refer to security incidents that occurred in the past.

- Check how information security incidents are collected and stored.

Annex 17: Information Security Aspects of Business Continuity Management

Business continuity during crises or adverse conditions like disasters can be lifesaving. The risk associated with business continuity is essential. The following points can help you identify gaps:

- Check whether business service continuity plans (for disasters like floods, earthquakes, fires, etc.) are defined and implemented.

- Check whether a policy is defined and documented to implement information security continuity.

- Check that your organization is verifying, reviewing, and evaluating information security continuity on a regular basis as per the defined policy if any.

- Check whether information-processing facilities are redundant to ensure failover from one component to another.

Annex 18: Compliance

This control emphasizes the need to maintain compliance requirements to prevent breaches of legal, statutory, regulatory, or contractual requirements. The following points can help you identify the gaps:

- Check whether all applicable legislation and contractual requirements have been identified for each location, country, etc.

- Check whether procedures are defined to prevent the misuse of intellectual property rights.

- Check which practices are implemented to protect and maintain the various record types that are generated.

- Check which practices are implemented to protect the privacy and protection of personally identifiable information.

- Check that the usage of cryptographic controls comply with all the relevant legislation and regulation.

- Check whether independent security reviews are conducted from time to time.

- Check how department managers conduct reviews of the defined policies and procedures from time to time.

- Check whether technical compliance reviews are planned and conducted from time to time to ensure that various hardware and software security controls are implemented in the right manner.

The purpose of explaining the controls from Annex 5 to Annex 18 is to help you easily understand them and be able to identify the gaps in your current practices,. which can further help you identify the initial risk assessment. You will read more about them in coming chapters, where you will read the detailed control execution.

Preparing the Analysis Report

So far, you have done the risk assessment exercise by meeting all the teams. Now it is time to prepare the report based on the identified gaps. This will tell you the level of control you have already implemented and are following, but will also show the areas that need work (gaps). The report acts as a picture of every department based on the international standard practices.

Figure 4-1 illustrates a sample analysis report for human resource security. The gap identification is classified in red, amber, and green areas, where red indicates the control is not implemented, amber indicates the control is partially implemented, and green indicates the control is fully implemented.

SAMPLE GAP ANALYSIS REPORT

A.7	Human resource security		
A.7.1	Prior to employment		
Objective: To ensure that employees and contractors understand their responsibilities and are suitable for the roles for which they are considered.			
A.7.1.1	Screening	Control Background verification checks on all candidates for employment shall be carried out in accordance with relevant laws, regulations and ethics and shall be proportional to the business requirements, the classification of the information to be accessed and the perceived risks.	NOT IMPLEMENTED
A.7.1.2	Terms and conditions of employment	Control The contractual agreements with employees and contractors shall state their and the organization's responsibilities for information security.	PARTIAL IMPLEMENTED
A.7.2	During employment		
Objective: To ensure that employees and contractors are aware of and fulfil their information security responsibilities.			
A.7.2.1	Management responsibilities	Control Management shall require all employees and contractors to apply information security in accordance with the established policies and procedures of the organization.	PARTIAL IMPLEMENTED
A.7.2.2	Information security awareness, education and training	Control All employees of the organization and, where relevant, contractors shall receive appropriate awareness education and training and regular updates in organizational policies and procedures, as relevant for their job function.	IMPLEMENTED
A.7.2.3	Disciplinary process	Control There shall be a formal and communicated disciplinary process in place to take action against employees who have committed an information security breach.	IMPLEMENTED
A.7.3	Termination and change of employment		
Objective: To protect the organization's interests as part of the process of changing or terminating employment.			
A.7.3.1	Termination or change of employment responsibilities	Control Information security responsibilities and duties that remain valid after termination or change of employment shall be defined, communicated to the employee or contractor and enforced.	NOT IMPLEMENTED

Figure 4-1. *Sample gap analysis report*

Now for every department and all the controls, you can depict in the same manner as shown for the HR control. This will act as a gap analysis report with the risks to work on.

Presenting the Report to Management/Teams

Once the report is ready, you must plan a session and present the report to the steering committee. It's important to get their opinion and support about the risks that the analysis classified as major. It is very important to know what your management's expectations are. The steering committee will be interested in knowing where the gaps exist in the system and what is required to close them. Some businesses are critical, and any open gaps can hamper their business in a way that's difficult to recover from. Hence critical gaps must not be hidden from the steering committee. For example, medical and defense organizations cannot keep gaps open for very long.

Once management sees this report, it will also act as an action tracker with target dates. The steering committee will be interested in knowing the timeline for each department to close their gaps, as shown in Figure 4-2. Any concern at this time must be discussed openly with management, as any concern not discussed here can become an issue in the future and management may not support that.

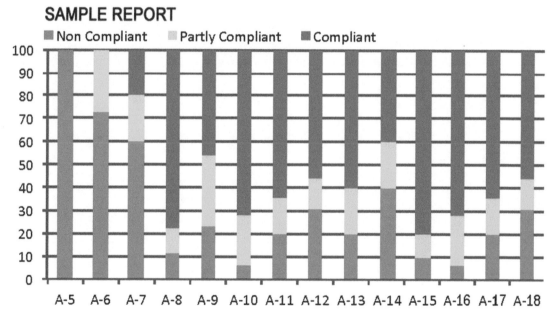

Figure 4-2. *Sample finding chart of control groups*

Summary

This chapter talked about how to conduct the initial risk assessment with all the teams and what to check for as a part of controls in the standard. You also learned that the analysis report is important from a management perspective, as management wants to know the areas with gaps. This report will also track actions for everyone.

CHAPTER 5

Risk Management Approach

"If you don't invest in risk management, it doesn't matter what business you're in, it's a risky business."

—Gary Cohn

The previous chapter discussed how to conduct a risk assessment exercise and give a risk assessment report presentation. This chapter discusses the approach to be followed for managing the risks identified during the risk assessment exercise. This chapter will also focus on identifying assets and applying security controls.

Defining and Finalizing the Risk Assessment Framework

When you initiate the risk assessment, it is important to identify the framework to be followed to manage risk. This method can help the teams provide a guideline to conduct a risk analysis on assets based on the defined scope.

There are three main scenarios for performing the risk assessment, which are as follows:

- Security risks must be unique and might lead to significant losses, if they occur.

- Organizations must comply with legal, statutory, and contractual requirements.

- Organizations must define objectives to support their business operations.

© Abhishek Chopra, Mukund Chaudhary 2020
A. Chopra and M. Chaudhary, *Implementing an Information Security Management System*,
https://doi.org/10.1007/978-1-4842-5413-4_5

It is also important to understand the benefits of conducting the risk assessment:

- Asset identification and its related vulnerabilities and security controls

- Decision making to rectify the risk

- Reason to spend budget expenditures for security implementation

- Help in improving awareness about information security

Figure 5-1 shows a high-level diagram for the risk framework.

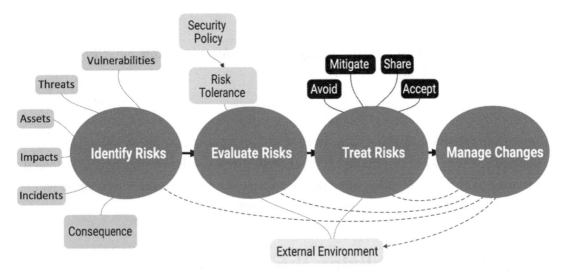

Figure 5-1. *A high-level risk framework*

Risk Components

The risk assessment process consists of the following components:

- Assets

- Threats

- Vulnerabilities

- Impact

- Probability of occurrence

- Consequences

Note   Most companies do not consider risk assessment for an asset value that is less than or equal to 5, as the impact to the business would be minimal or negligible.

What Are Threats?

In ISO 27001, the term "threat" is designed to focus on identifying and analyzing scenarios that are unexpected or unwanted, and if they occurred, would cause harm to the organization. Risk assessment is based on threat identification, which means if there is a potential scenario of a threat, you need to do risk analysis or assessment and treatment.

A threat may be caused by intentional or unintentional acts. There are also acts of nature, such as floods, fires, and earthquakes, which you cannot control.

There are different types of threats, and each threat could lead to unique problems. Some examples are:

- Asset may malfunction or be damaged

- Asset may be corrupted or modified

- Asset may be stolen or lost

- Asset may be disclosed to unauthorized people

- Any other interruption of services

What Are Vulnerabilities?

A "vulnerability" is a weakness in an asset or system that makes it susceptible to threats.

For example, if you are vulnerable to a specific type of allergy, it's because your immune system reacts to that particular allergen. To avoid this issue, you can either take steps to make your body strong or avoid certain actions to prevent interacting with this allergen.

When you come across a condition or set of conditions that occurs frequently in your business operations and exploits an asset, you need to identify the vulnerability and avoid the conditions.

Note   It is important to identify vulnerabilities as early as possible. By analyzing conditions in which you can use the asset, you should collect and analyze various other inputs, such as reports and penetration tests, which may provide better understanding in identifying vulnerabilities.

What Is a Security Risk?

How do you define a security risk? When you get input by analyzing a threat to an asset and determine the associated vulnerabilities, you will arrive at a conclusion. If the identified threat has the potential to exploit any vulnerabilities and negatively impact an asset or group of assets, that constitutes a security risk. This means directly or indirectly there will be a negative impact on your organization.

You also need to evaluate the security risk level in order to identify which security risk:

- May have the biggest impact

- Needs to be addressed first

- Can be put under a watch list and addressed later

To determine the risk value, you combine the asset values (covered in the "Asset Value" section of this chapter), the assessed levels of risk, and the risk's impact.

The formula is as follows:

Risk Value = Asset Value * Likelihood * Impact

Table 5-1 shows the risk likelihood levels, rating levels, and their descriptions.

Table 5-1. *Risk Likelihood Level and Rating*

Likelihood Levels	Rating	Description
Rare	1	Very low probability of occurrence (might occur once every 3-4 years or more) Might cause a very negligible impact
Moderate	2	Might occur every two years Has a noticeable impact, i.e., some financial loss or data loss may occur
Likely	3	Might occur at least once a year Has a significant impact, i.e., financial loss or data loss or could be injuries to people and other assets
Almost Certain	4	Might occur more than once a year Has a very high impact, i.e., financial loss or data loss or could be injuries to people and other assets

Table 5-2 shows the risk impact rating levels and their descriptions.

Table 5-2. *Risk Impact Ratings*

Impact Scale	Rating	Description
Minor	1	Service or business downtime that is less than a few hours (for IT infrastructure and other operational facilities)
Moderate	2	Service or business downtime that is more than a few hours and could last for one calendar day
Major	3	Service or business downtime that is more than a day and could affect delivery of services, so that the office/site is not operational (could be for hours or days) Or, the IT infrastructure is down or not able to reach the office/site due to public strikes, floods, earthquakes, etc.
Catastrophic	4	Service or business downtime caused by severe damage to the office/site and the IT infrastructure Major financial loss leading to operations being shut down

What Is a Risk Ranking?

The rank assigned to each risk is called its risk ranking. Risks are ranked into four types, depending on the calculated risk value and the priority level of the risk.

Table 5-3 shows the risk rankings and a description of the associated actions that could be taken to treat the risks.

Table 5-3. *Risk Rankings*

Risk Value	Risk Rank	Description	Risk Priority
1 – 36	Low	A security control already exists Chance to exploit the vulnerability is low Requires monitoring	P4
37 – 72	Medium	There are chances to exploit the vulnerability Probability of occurrence is medium May damage only non-critical application/services and associated assets. No major impact but proactive risk monitoring is required	P3
73 - 108	High	There are high chances to exploit the vulnerability Probability of occurrence is high May impact critical business applications or services resulting in service degradation High impact on business operations and risk monitoring is required on regular/frequent basis	P2
109 - 144	Very High	There are very high chances to exploit the vulnerability Probability of occurrence is very high Adverse impact on critical business applications/services resulting in major downtime of services Very high impact on business operations and risk monitoring is required on regular/frequent basis	P1

Risk Prioritization

Table 5-4 shows the actions that can be taken based on each risk priority ranking. The idea is to prioritize the risks and to allocate resources appropriately for risk treatment.

Table 5-4. *Risk Prioritization*

Risk Priority	Action
P1	Risk is a showstopper or blocker
	Plan for immediate action
	Actions taken must bring down the risk to an acceptable level
P2	Take actions mentioned in Table 5-3
P3	Take actions mentioned in Table 5-3
P4	No action required

After analyzing the risk ranking for each risk, the focus should be to reduce the priority ranking of the risks to P4. It is not always possible to reduce the risk priority, as situations will not always be in your control. Thus, in those scenarios, you should document the justifications for not being able to reduce the risk. It is important to present such scenarios to management and seek their approval to avoid any confusion later.

Risk Owner Identification

It is the responsibility of each department head to take ownership of their departmental risks. Then they can assign further risk ownership to their team members. Once all the risk owners have been identified, they can start analyzing the risks and evaluate them based on the risk acceptance criteria defined in their organization.

Risk Treatment

Risk owners and teams need to analyze which risks are acceptable and which risks require immediate attention. Risk decisions fall into one of the following:

- Risk acceptance
- Risk mitigation
- Risk avoidance
- Risk transfer

Risk Acceptance

To decide whether to accept the risk or not, you should focus on the following implementation constraints:

- *Budget/financial:* Financial constraints may force management to reject the budget so the security control cannot be implemented.

- *Environmental:* Environmental factors such as space availability at the office/site, climate conditions, and surrounding natural and geographical conditions can all affect the decision process.

- *Organizational:* Some measures are not feasible to implement due to organizational constraints.

- *Technological:* Some technology is not feasible to implement, as it's incompatible with the current hardware and software setup.

- *Cultural:* Implemented security controls can be ineffective if staff or clients/stakeholders do not accept them due to cultural norms or taboos.

- *Time-based:* It takes time to implement any control. Thus, sometimes you may need to wait for the budget or for the right opportunity to act.

  - *Not Applicable:* Sometimes, the organization doesn't think their business operation is big enough, or they may not be processing highly sensitive data and therefore they don't want to implement the security control.

  - *Personnel:* The resources or staff needed is currently unavailable so the security control cannot be planned.

  - *Legal:* Sometimes legal constraints stand in the way of implementing the controls.

Note   There may be other reasons for not implementing the controls, other than those listed here. It depends on your business and industry requirements.

Risk Mitigation

Mitigation in simple terms involves the planned and executed actions you take to reduce the impact of any risk.

In ISO 27001, risk reduction is done when you select the controls to be implemented for the assessed risks. You select these controls from the ISO 27001 standard implementation guide, which helps you achieve the desired result and in turn reduces the risk. Some of the criteria to consider are as follows:

- *Threat reduction*, to reduce the probability of a threat from occurring.

- *Vulnerability reduction*, to reduce or remove a vulnerability.

- *Impact reduction*, to reduce the impact of a security breach to an acceptable level.

- *Detection of unwanted event*, to determine whether a threat is easily detectable or identifiable.

- *Recovery from unwanted event*, to recover from the event, thereby reducing the impact.

The control is selected based on the assurance provided by treating the risk and the acceptable (residual) risk after implementing that control. The Information Security team should review and approve the selected controls.

As part of implementing security controls to treat risks, risk owners can take the following actions:

- Acquire the required systems

- Develop or modify policies

- Develop procedures and practices

Risk Avoidance

Risk avoidance is possible when potential threats are eliminated. This is often done by changing process ladders or execution methods. For example, instead of using foreign vendors, local vendors are used, as the risk of using them is much less.

Tip   Risk owners must review risks that fall under the category of risk avoidance with the Information Security/compliance team and any relevant stakeholders.

Risk Transfer

This is often the best strategy, as organizations can share their risk burdens with third parties on contractual terms.

Note   All contractual terms must be clearly identified in the agreement before proceeding with a third party.

For example, you can insure business-critical assets by purchasing an insurance policy. Thus, if an event occurs, the insurance policy will help manage costs, such as repairs, lost expenses, legal expenses, etc.

Another example is outsourcing business processes to third parties due to lack of experience/skills in-house. In this case, risk could be minimized, as the third party provides the assurance that outsourced processes will be taken care of.

Caution   Be sure to review risk transfer cases with the Information Security team and to get approval from management before making a final decision.

What Is Acceptable Risk?

What is acceptable risk? In other words, how much risk can an organization accept?

Acceptable risk is the risk that remains or still exists after implementing security controls. Table 5-5 describes the different kinds of acceptable risk.

Table 5-5.   *Acceptable Risk*

Acceptable Risk	Description
Very High/High/Medium	Requires additional controls to bring the risk to an acceptable level It should be accepted only if management approves it
Low	Risk is at an acceptable level

Note   When the risk score is higher than the acceptable level, the controls must be analyzed again and re-implemented.

Risk Monitoring and Review

Risk monitoring and review is a continuous process. Once you implement the security measures and controls, you must monitor and track the progress of all risks on a regular basis to ensure you're getting the desired result. Risk owners from their respective departments are also responsible for monitoring and reviewing risks and reporting to management on a monthly basis (or as needed).

Identifying Assets

Before you start learning how to identify information assets based on the ISO 27001 implementation, it is important to understand what is meant by assets.

An *asset* can be anything that has value to the organization. This can be tangible or intangible value. For example, machines, people, software, patents, reputation, etc. Assets include all those items that contribute to the establishment of information that an organization requires to conduct their daily business operations.

From an information security point of view, an asset can be any device, data, or components of environments such as development, testing, and production environments that support the information security activities within the organization. In general terms, anything that you see in your organization that helps or supports the day-to-day activities, using assets such as laptops, desktops, hardware (servers, switches, and routers), software (business and/or support applications and software tools), and any confidential information (trade secrets and financial data).

Table 5-6 shows a comprehensive list asset register that you should prepare.

Table 5-6. *Asset Register Categorization*

Asset	Category
Information assets	Include files including details, image files, product information, manuals, policies, and procedures
Paper assets	Include HR records, contracts, invoices and, written papers
Software assets	Include system software, application software, and development tools and utilities that are required
Hardware/physical assets	Include computer and communications equipment, magnetic media, environmental equipment, furniture, facilities, accommodations, etc.
Extension services	Include communication services, air conditioning, lighting, UPS, generators, service providers, etc.
People assets	Include employees, contractors, visitors, guests, etc.

Asset Value

Each asset is assigned a value, called the asset value. In simple terms, this helps you decide the importance of the asset to your business and its operations. The asset value helps you identify and determine the appropriate protection for the assets. You can also use asset values to identify and describe the consequences that might occur if an unexpected event occurred.

In Table 5-7, the criticality rating is defined at three levels. This rating is based on the confidentiality, integrity, and availability of an asset. These numbers represent how critical an asset is to the business.

Table 5-7. *Criticality Ratings*

Rating	Information Asset Security Elements		
	Confidentiality (C)	Integrity (I)	Availability (A)
1	Public	Low	Not Important
2	Internal	Medium	Important
3	Confidential	High	Very Important

By using the rating formula, you can calculate the net asset value of an asset. The net asset value is the sum of the confidentiality, integrity, and availability values.

Net Asset Value = (Confidentiality + Integrity + Availability)

For example, say you are calculating an asset value for the HR data. The confidentiality = 2, the integrity = 3, and the availability = 1. In that case, the net asset value would be: 2+3+1 = 6. So, the asset value of that HR data is 6.

Asset Classification

An asset can be grouped into different categories based on similarities and characteristics. The process of grouping similar assets is called *asset classification*.

For example, servers, routers, switches, and LAN cables can be grouped as IT assets. Desktops, VDI devices, and IP phones can be added into the IT asset group, or you are free to make a new sub-category for these assets.

Note   Asset classification varies from organization to organization and the industry to industry. The grouping of assets depends on the asset owners.

Figure 5-2 shows data classifications, which will help you protect information access.

Data Classsifications

Figure 5-2. *Data classification*

Asset Labeling

Once you are done with the information asset classification process, it must be labeled properly. You need to determine how your team will label the assets. Asset labeling is the small step toward achieving better security, since organizations deal with lots of information assets in their daily activities. That means the chances of misplacing or losing assets or if them being stolen is greater. Therefore, asset tagging or labeling is very important in order to cut down on administrative expenses.

There is no one good way to do asset labeling. You can use unique asset identification numbers or codes or indicate details about the specific location or group, or use any other relevant asset category. These labels can be QR codes, bar codes, or RFIDs. These codes can be easily scanned to provide additional information about the asset, which makes it easier to monitor and track the assets.

Any asset that you think is crucial to your business needs to be labeled. Each asset should have a different identifier, such as a serial number or an asset identification number (AIN). See Figure 5-3 as an example.

Note   There is no specific format for tagging assets. They should be tagged based on your defined organizational procedure. Some companies prefer not to mention the company name when tagging the assets, for security purposes.

Some best practices for labeling assets include:

- *By item ID:* Some assets are tagged based on their IDs or location. For example, if your company is in New Delhi and you are tagging a laptop from the software team, you can code it as follows. ND is for New Delhi. For laptops, you can assign a sequential code L001 to L00N based on the number of laptops you have. Then you include a department ID. For the software department, let's say the ID is S01. The final code would be ND/L001/S01 or ND-L001-S01.

Tip   This labeling practice is best suited if your employees tend to travel with their tools or machines or you have multiple departments in your organization.

- *Adding a color code:* In some cases, item ID tagging will not work. For example, companies with different software teams working on different software projects demand different configuration needs for their projects. In such scenarios, adding color codes to the asset will be helpful. Laptops with a high configuration can tagged with blue, a middle configuration with green, and those with a basic configuration can be tagged with amber to differentiate them. Similarly, tags can be used for LAN cables for voice data, browsing data, and lease lines.

- *Customized tagging:* The need for tagging depends on the categories of assets that you want to tag. Hence, customized tagging is also important. For example, you want to label the information using barcodes that may contain different data as per your business needs. This could include manufacturer name, manufacture year, serial number, or other tracking numbers.

Note   Barcodes and QR codes are very popular these days. Based on the report published in an EZOfficeInventory whitepaper, use of asset tags can reduce administrative errors by up to 41.4%.

Source: https://www.ezofficeinventory.com/

Figure 5-3. *Asset labeling*

So far so good. These are just some of the benefits of asset labeling:

- Stock availability

- Tracking

- Better monitoring

Asset Register

An *asset register* is a list of assets owned by the organization. The main benefit of having an asset register is that it gives you a list of assets along with their owners. Every department needs to create an asset register.

To create the register, you need to identify the various assets in the business' operations and in its daily activities. This can sometimes be tedious to identify. Table 5-8 shows some of the examples of assets in different sub-groups and categories that might help you identify assets more easily.

Table 5-8. *Assets in Different Sub-Groups and Categories*

Hardware/Physical Assets	Software
Computers	Anti-virus software
Servers	Business applications
Switches/routers/hubs	Network management system software
Access points	Development tools
Access card readers	Operating systems
Firewalls	Utilities
Communication equipment	
Data storage	
Cabinets	
Safes	
Server racks	
Services	**People**
Outsourced operations	Employees
Outsourced services	Customers
Outsourced telephone operations	Subscribers
Security services	Contracts
IT services	
Information	**Paper**
Databases and data files/soft copies	Contracts
System documentation/manual	HR records
User manuals	Invoices
Training materials	
Operational or support procedures	
Backup	
AMC document	

Asset Disposal

Asset disposal is the act of obsoleting unwanted equipment or assets in a safe manner. A large volume of data is being transferred and stored on computer systems and the security of this information is essential, even when the data is being removed. If the information is not properly removed before the disposal of asset, it could be accessed and viewed by unauthorized personnel.

Hence, organizations need to write an organizational policy that covers the disposal of information assets. A few key points that need to be covered in this asset disposable policy are the following:

- *Media sanitization procedures:* All the electronic media must be properly sanitized before it is transferred from the custody of its current owner. The proper sanitization method depends on the type of media and the intended disposal process of the media. For example, if you are sharing the hard drive from one department to another, it must be formatted before being reused to ensure security of the data.

- *Destruction of electronic media:* Destruction of electronic media is the process of physically damaging the medium so that it cannot be reused by any device that may normally be used to read electronic information, such as computers, hard drives, pen drives, etc.

- *Repairing hard drives under warranty:* In a special situation where a hard drive under warranty has failed and the manufacturer requires that the failed disk drive be returned, an appropriate Business Associate Agreement between the manufacturer and organization must be in place before the drive can be shipped to the manufacturer. If the manufacturer will not sign a Business Associate Agreement, the old drive must be properly destroyed.

- *Disposal of damaged media:* The first attempt should be to overwrite the hard drive or other media device. If it cannot be overwritten, the hard drive must be disassembled and mechanically destroyed so that it is not usable.

- *External party:* You can choose from many companies that will remove your media, but you need to make sure that the provider you select agrees to the non-disclosure agreement (NDA) and follows it.

The disposal of media is very essential and not hard work if you follow these simple steps.

Tip   An organization may use a shredder to destroy any important physical information. It's a very secure and cost-effective way to dispose of information.

Asset Register Examples

This section explains how to track and maintain asset information in your department, with examples. The following sections discuss some examples of departments.

Human Resources Department

In any organization, human resources is the first department that communicates the company's information security controls and ensures that everybody follows them.

Figure 5-4 shows the sample HR assets. There could be more, depending on the organization. For example, this register should include any software application/tool used by HR to perform HR operations.

The two important columns in the table to note are Category and Asset Value. The Category column determines whether the information is in the form of paper or soft copy. Assets like laptops or desktops are common in each department, so they fall under the Hardware/Physical category. People are also assets, so team members fall under the People category. Some documents are for information purposes only, so they can be placed in the Information category.

Human Resource						Asset Owner	<Name>
						Risk Owner	<Name>
Asset Register							
S.No.	Asset Name	Category	Confidentiality	Integrity	Availability	Asset Value	Justification for Asset Vallue
1	laptops	Hardware-Physical	3	2	1	6	
2	Desktops	Hardware-Physical	3	3	1	7	
3	HR records	Paper	3	2	3	8	
4	Invoices	Paper	3	3	1	7	
5	Employee Offer Letters	Paper	3	2	3	8	
6	Employee Handbook	Information	2	2	1	5	
7	Head of Department	People	3	3	2	8	

Figure 5-4. *HR asset register*

The second most important thing in this table is the Asset Value. The Asset Value column in Figure 5-4 shows numbers, which are calculated by taking the sum of the values of Confidentiality, Integrity, and Availability. If the sum value is more than 5, it becomes important and you must implement controls. Note the Justification for Asset Value column. It is good to provide reasons in your own words so that nobody questions the given asset's value.

Note   For each department, the asset value will be different. The importance of an asset may vary from department to department because they process and store different information.

The Asset, Category, and Asset Value columns must be filled in for each department involved in the ISO 27001 implementation journey. Some of the assets could be similar, but the data processed or stored by them could be different and their purposes could differ too.

IT Helpdesk Department

Whatever you call the IT support department, their functions and activities will basically be the same. This department typically covers about 30-40% of the ISO 27001 security controls implementation. The IT helpdesk department usually takes care of the following assets:

- Laptops/desktops allotment and maintenance
- Software licenses and installation
- Network services management
- Antivirus protection
- Email configuration/email server management and backup
- Printer configuration and maintenance

Based on this asset list, the IT asset register can be prepared similar to the HR asset register shown in Figure 5-4.

IT Infrastructure Department

Whatever you call the IT infrastructure department, their functions and activities will basically be the same. This department typically covers about 20-30% of the ISO 27001 security controls implementation.

The IT infrastructure department usually takes care of the following assets:

- Server management

    - Installation

    - Maintenance

    - Data backup

- Software licenses and installation

Based on this asset list, you can create an asset register for the IT infrastructure department.

The next section looks at the other important operations, services, and departments.

Software Development Department

In any organization, the software development division is crucial, as throughout the software development lifecycle, they handle the information related to their client's product and software development. Hence, the business analyst, architecture, developer, and tester teams are all involved.

The software division takes care of the following assets:

- Requirement documents

- Architecture/design documents

- Software code

- Test documents

Similarly, based on this asset list, you can prepare the asset register for the software development team.

From the asset register examples, you should now understand how to identify the assets of any department. Remember the most important thing, which is to ask what information does that department process and store. This will make asset identification a lot easier.

By using the examples in this chapter, you should be able to identify the critical assets in any organization, whether it is in IT/software, IT/call center, manufacturing, or any other industry.

Managing Risks

In the previous chapter, you performed an initial risk assessment. If you remember, each department risk owner analyzed key questions about the information assets to determine "the current/existing controls which are already in place" for the risks identified. If you stop there, you see from Figure 5-5 what it takes to fill this information into the risk assessment tracker.

Figure 5-5 shows the risk assessment tracker's columns. Let's look at the columns covered in more detail:

- *Department*: Enter the name of the department for which the tracker is being filled, such as HR.

- *Asset*: The name of the asset being tracked, such as laptop.

- *Category*: The category of the asset. The laptop category, for example, is Hardware-Physical.

- *Asset value:* The value of the asset, as explained earlier in the chapter. The laptop's asset value, for example, is 9, which is more than 5.

- *Threat*: The threat related to this asset, as explained earlier in the chapter.

- *Vulnerability*: Any vulnerability related to this asset, as explained earlier in the chapter.

- *Risk*: The risk description, which explains what the risk is.

- *Likelihood*: A rating on a scale of 1 to 4 that communicates the chances of this risk occurring. 1 is least likely and 4 is most likely. (This assumes no security controls have been implemented.)

- *Impact*: The impact of this risk if it were to occur. You need to rate it on a scale of 1 to 4. 1 is the least impact and 4 is the highest impact. (This assumes no security controls have been implemented.)

- *Risk value*: Calculated by multiplying the Asset Value∗Likelihood Rating∗Impact Rating. (This assumes no security controls have been implemented.)

- *Risk rank:* The risk rank will be populated based on the risk value range. Hence, you add a formula to your assessment tracker for the risk rank column.

- *Risk priority:* The priority of the risk as explained earlier in this chapter. You put a formula in your assessment tracker for the risk priority column.

- *Risk owner:* List the owner of the risk, which is who will handle the risk mitigation process. Note in Figure 5-5 that the risk mentioned is the HR department, but the risk owner is the IT manager. This is because security control implementation comes under the IT helpdesk department. Hence, you need to identify the right risk owner.

- *Existing controls:* Mention any security controls that are already implemented for this risk. If there are no controls implemented, enter "there are no existing controls".

Note   In the table in Figure 5-5, all the information is filled out on the basis that no security controls have been implemented.

Risk Identification						Inherent risk (Risks without any controls)							
Department	Asset	Category	Asset value (AV)	Threats	Vulnerability	Risk	Likelihood (L)	Impact (I)	Risk Value (RV) (AV*L*I)	Risk Rank	Risk Priority	Risk Owner	Existing Controls
HR & Admin	laptops	Hardware-Physical	9	unauthorized use	lack of access control policy	Unauthorized use of laptop can lead unauthorized access, modification, deletion of critical information.	2	4	72	Medium	P3	IT Manager	1. Laptop and computer usage/ computer and Internet usage policy is in place. 2. Confidentiality agreement is singed by employee 3. Password management is in place. 4. Backup has been taken on regular basis.
HR & Admin	laptops	Hardware-Physical	9	Theft or loss	Lack of Hard disk encryption	Laptops contain all employee related confidential /Sensitive information. Since Laptop's are not encrypted, there is a high chance of these data could be misused in the event of theft / loss.	2	4	72	Medium	P3	IT Manager	1. Laptop and computer usage policy is in place. 2. Backup taken on regular basis. 3. Physical security controls are in place.

Figure 5-5. *The first 14 columns of the risk assessment tracker*

When you move ahead from the Existing Controls column, you need to enter the calculated Risk Value and Risk Rank (see Figure 5-6). These help you determine whether the existing controls are enough to manage the risk at present or whether you need to identify and implement additional security controls.

Note that Figure 5-6 shows the same risk as Figure 5-5. You need to again add the likelihood and impact ratings to calculate the risk value and risk rank, but this time considering the risk treatment with existing controls. Hence, if the risk rank is low, you don't have to identify a new control. But if the risk rank is medium or high, you must identify and recommend new controls.

Risk Identification				Inherent risk (Risks without any controls)			Risks with existing treatment				
Department	Asset	Category	Asset value (AV)	Threats	Vulnerability	Risk	Existing Controls	Likelihood (L)	Impact (I)	Risk Value (RV) (AV*L*I)	Risk Rank
HR & Admin	laptops	Hardware-Physical	9	unauthorized use	lack of access control policy	Unauthorized use of laptop can lead unauthorized access, modification, deletion of critical information.	1. Laptop and computer usage/ computer and internet usage policy is in place. 2. Confidentiality agreement is singed by employee 3. Password management is in place. 4. Backup has been taken on regular basis.	1	2	18	Low
HR & Admin	laptops	Hardware-Physical	9	Theft or loss	Lack of Hard disk encryption	Laptops contain all employee related confidential /Sensitive information. Since Laptop's are not encrypted, there is a high chance of these data could be misused in the event of theft / loss.	1. Laptop and computer usage policy is in place. 2. Backup taken on regular basis. 3. Physical security controls are in place.	2	4	72	Medium

Figure 5-6. *An extended column of the risk assessment tracker*

Hence, these steps for managing risks constitute a common method for implementation in departments and organizations. Every risk should be managed and tracked under the risk assessment tracker. The format of the risk tracker could be a little different in some organizations, but the basic setup of the tracker will essentially be the same.

Note   Organizations that are new to information security and have fewer existing controls in place might need to identify more security controls than organizations that are more aware or mature.

Identifying Security Controls

Along with managing risks, you need to start identifying the appropriate security controls. They should be based on the risk value/risk rank, in order to mitigate the risks and minimize the impact of the threats you identified based on the risk assessment exercise.

It is important to remember that you need to identify meaningful controls, as this will help you achieve the desired result, which is to protect the information from getting stolen, destroyed, or modified. If the identified control is not helping, you need to change the strategy as needed.

This section outlines some examples of security controls.

Note it is the same risk as shown in Figures 5-5 and 5-6. In the example in Figure 5-7, where the risk rank is Medium, the controls listed there should be implemented. The recommended mitigation method becomes Address, which means the controls should be implemented to address this risk. The proposed mitigation plan should be implemented at the departmental or organizational level. To this kind of tracker, you can also add and track target dates for the mitigation plan.

Risk Identification			Inherent risk (Risks without any controls)				Risks with existing treatment			Control Recommendation		
Department	Asset	Category	Asset value (AV)	Threats	Vulnerability	Risk	Existing Controls	Risk Value (RV) (AV*L*1)	Risk Rank	Identified controls	Recommended Mitigation Method	Proposed Mitigation plan
HR & Admin	laptops	Hardware-Physical	9	unauthorized use	lack of access control policy	Unauthorized use of laptop can lead unauthorized access, modification, deletion of critical information.	1. Laptop and computer usage/ computer and internet usage policy is in place. 2. Confidentiality agreement is singed by employee 3. Password management is in place. 4. Backup has been taken on regular basis.	18	Low	No further controls recommended at this point of time	Accept	
HR & Admin	laptops	Hardware-Physical	9	Theft or loss	Lack of Hard disk encryption	Laptops contain all employee related confidential /Sensitive information. Since Laptop's are not encrypted, there is a high chance of these data could be misused in the event of theft / loss.	1. Laptop and computer usage policy is in place. 2. Backup taken on regular basis. 3. Physical security controls are in place.	72	Medium	Protection of data stored in these laptops should be ensured through disk level encryption so that, even if the laptop is stolen or lost; data could not be retrieved by unauthorized people.	Address	all critical latops needs to be enabled with Bitlocker Encryption.

Figure 5-7. *Security controls are identified and recommendations are listed*

Revisiting the Statement of Applicability (SoA)

You may wonder why you need to revisit the SoA, as you already did so in an earlier exercise. Recall from an earlier chapter that you learned that you might have to revisit the SoA, as when you proceed with the implementation, you may find areas or scenarios that were skipped. In those cases, you need to modify the SoA document, which helps to clarify the scope for the implementation and the certification audit.

Thus, at this stage, it's smart to analyze the SoA again and determine whether any changes are required or not.

Summary

This chapter covered the risk management approach, including the following topics:

- Risk framework: This is important from the perspective of setting a clear path to manage risks. Once the path is set, it becomes easier to move forward.

- Asset management: You learned how to identify assets, about the different types of assets, and how to maintain and dispose of them. By understanding assets, you can manage the asset lifecycle more easily.

- Manage risks and identify controls: You learned how you need to manage risks and identify suitable controls on the path of implementation. This is an important practical step, as it helps to check whether the implementation is accurate.

- Revisit the Statement of Applicability (SoA): You learned about the need for revisiting the SoA.

CHAPTER 6

Execution

"Success doesn't necessarily come from breakthrough innovation but from flawless execution. A great strategy alone won't win a game or a battle; the win comes from basic blocking and tackling."

—Naveen Jain

This chapter covers what all can be implemented as part of the execution. You'll see examples of all the controls that can be implemented based on the practices/procedures followed in your organization.

Information Security Awareness

Why is security awareness important at this stage? Awareness of the ISO 27001 standard should be planned and conducted at the organizational level. This is because when the implementation is in progress, it will help employees to understand what is being implemented in terms of security controls, as well as why they are being implemented and what the associated benefits are.

Most organizations only educate their implementation team members about the security implementation and never reach all the employees. This could be because management/senior members may not know the importance or there might be operational issues. But it's important to realize that the employees must be aware of the importance of safeguarding information/assets and sometimes they are the ones who unknowingly cause security breaches.

© Abhishek Chopra, Mukund Chaudhary 2020
A. Chopra and M. Chaudhary, *Implementing an Information Security Management System*,
https://doi.org/10.1007/978-1-4842-5413-4_6

Hence, planning these awareness sessions is important, regardless of your size. In big organizations, awareness sessions can be planned in batches. Information security must take attendance from all the employees/attendees to ensure all employees are covered as part of the exercise. If some employees are absent or on official travel, they must be covered in other batches/sessions.

In some organizations, contractors/vendors are also part of the workforce, so they must also attend the awareness sessions. They need to be familiar with the security policies and need to abide by them. Any support staff, for example, cleaning staff, security guards, car drivers, and so on, who work inside and outside the premises must know their information security responsibilities.

An Emphasis on Training Content

It is important to know what you are covering as part of the awareness content. It should be easy for all employees to understand and they must remember them as well. After the awareness sessions, you need to collect feedback from the employees, and this will help you understand whether they have understood or not. That way, you can improve the content accordingly.

Note   Awareness training content can be reviewed periodically to ensure that the training content is effective and easy to understand.

Awareness Quiz

A quiz session makes the awareness training more interesting and attendees get to play a game and learn at the same time. This is the best way to check whether employees understood the awareness sessions. The quiz can be easily created online for all your staff members to take at the same time, or they can be given a timeframe to complete the quiz.

Quiz questions should be objective types with options. Keep the quiz to 10 or 15 questions, so employees don't feel overwhelmed when completing it. It should take up to five minutes to complete the quiz.

For each objective type, mark the points and decide on the passing score. Any employee who scores less than the passing score must retake the quiz. This process should continue for new employees as part of their induction.

Tip   Quizzes can be created offline or online as a part of the assessment. An online quiz can be more fun and create more interest, while offline quizzes are more of an assessment.

The awareness session also helps implementation team members when writing the policies and procedures. When the inputs are clear, it is easier to define them, and they will know how easily they will be understood by the employees when they read them.

Policies and Procedures

The most important step in the execution is defining the policy and operational procedures. Without them, the implementation will be incomplete. If you are going for an external audit, the auditor requires these procedures as part of the audit exercise to verify how they have defined and followed. Employees must adhere to the practices defined in the policy. These are the defined rules to be followed by all.

As part of the ISO 27001 standard implementation, you must define policies to cover various security controls, although the standard does not mandate standard operating procedures. Without having these procedures in place, your company won't achieve the desired result consistently every time. To avoid defining too many procedures in the ISO 27001 implementation, the policies cover how security controls/practices should be implemented in the organization or in one of the business units of the organization, as applicable.

Who Defines the Policies?

As mentioned, the applicable team members help define the policies that affect their daily work routines. It is the combination of the information security team and the members from the operational team who work together. The information security team acts as the subject matter experts (SMEs). They collect various inputs from the operation team to define policies, and once they are defined, they must be shared for review and approval.

Who Reviews and Approves the Policies?

The best way to go about this is to form a team of seniors (such as team heads and management) who will review and approve the policies, as they know the business processes very well and have the authority to change or modify them as needed. These are important reviews that need to be done before finalizing and rolling out the policies to all the employees. The final okay on the policies comes from management.

Note   Depending on the type of organization, management members' roles could be different, hence no specific designation is mentioned here. Organizations, based on their organization/team structure, should decide which management member will approve which policy.

Which Policies and Procedures Are Covered?

The following policies are examples based on the ISO 27001 standard. Organizations can prepare their policies as applicable.

- Access control policy
- Acceptable usage policy
- Asset management policy
- Antivirus policy
- Business continuity and data recovery policy
- Clear desk and clear screen policy
- Change management policy
- Data retention and disposal policy
- Email usage policy
- Encryption policy
- Information security policy
- Incident management policy

- Information classification policy

- Legal compliance policy

- Network security and information transfer policy

- Password creation policy

- Physical and environmental security policy

- Privacy and protection of personally identifiable information management policy

- Remote access policy

- Supplier relationship management policy

- Technical vulnerabilities management policy

The following is a standard operating procedures example list. Organizations should create their operational procedures based on their industry/domain and business model.

- Operational planning procedure

- Requirement collection/development procedure

- Operational design procedure

- Coding procedure (applicable to IT/software companies)

- Change management procedure

The following sections discuss each policy and procedure, one by one.

Access Control Policy

The main objective of the access control policy is to protect an organization's resources from unauthorized access while facilitating seamless and legitimate use of these resources. This policy document should cover both logical and physical access control. It should cover the following items:

- Policy on user account management:

  - Write a formal user registration and de-registration procedure for granting and revoking access to all information systems and services.

- Explain how access rights will be created for new joiners and which rights are provided to the users by default.

- Unique user IDs and passwords are assigned to enable users to be linked and held responsible for their actions.

- Privilege management covers the following:

  - Privileges should be allowed to users on a need-to-use basis and on an event-by-event basis in line with the access control policy.

  - The access privileges should be associated with each system product (e.g., operating systems or database management) and each application should be identified along with its users.

  - An authorization process should be in place and a record of all privileges allocated should be maintained and monitored. Privileges should not be granted until the authorization process is complete.

- Rules for physical access to the premises are defined here. A few examples are shared for understanding:

  - Employees are allowed on floors except the IT server room and management area.

  - The IT team can access all the areas (depending on the work).

  - Biometric access may be issued by the admin or HR department on the same day as joining.

Note   Other components can also be added, based on the organization and industry. The examples here are for illustrative purposes. They might not fit into every organization.

Acceptable Usages Policy

The main objective of the acceptable usages policy is to document and define the practices that users must agree to in order to access the organizational network or Internet. Some organizations require employees to accept this usages policy before they can access the network or Internet.

Here are some of the points to cover in this policy:

- Don't use any service as part of violating the rights of any person or company protected by copyrights, trade secrets, patents, and/or other intellectual property, or laws/regulations, including, but not limited to, the installation or distribution of "pirated" or other software products.

- Don't attempt to break the security of any computer network by introducing malicious programs into the network or server (e.g., viruses, worms, Trojan horses, email bombs, etc.).

- Don't use any program/script/command or send messages of any kind with the intent to interfere with, or disable, a user's terminal session, via any means, either locally or via the Internet.

- Don't send junk email or spam to anyone who doesn't want to receive it. For example, if individuals have requested they not receive material, you should not send them related emails.

- Don't send any form of harassment via email, telephone, or through any other means.

- Don't misuse any assets provided by the organization for personal use.

Asset Management Policy

This document describes the asset management policy for all IT and non-IT assets of the organization. The policy covers all information assets, such as hardware, software, and data. As the name suggests, the key component of this policy is management and it should cover:

- Identification and inventory of all the assets and relevant information about their location, backup, business value, criticality, etc. For example, these assets can be:

  - Information assets such as databases, contracts, agreements, manuals, policies, plans, etc.

  - Software assets such as system software, application software, utilities, etc.

- Hardware assets such as computer hardware, servers, communication services, removable media devices, etc.

- Personnel assets such as people, their qualifications, and the skills, etc.

- Every asset should have a designated owner, which could be a person, a business process, an application.

This covers the monitoring and tracking of all the assets during their lifespan with the organization.

Antivirus Policy

The purpose of this policy is to help prevent the infection by computers and other malicious code and to provide a virus-free environment. The goal is to prevent the organization's data from damage due to a virus/Trojan attack.

This policy should cover the following issues as a best practice:

- Antivirus software and virus pattern files must be kept up-to-date.

- Virus-infected computers must be removed from the network until they are verified as virus free or the machine has been reformatted, if possible.

- Do open any files or macros attached to an email from an unknown, suspicious, or untrustworthy source. It's best to delete these attachments immediately and remove them from the trash.

- Delete spam, chain, and other junk emails without forwarding them. Never download files from unknown or suspicious sources.

- Do not directly share reading/writing access to the disk unless there is a compelling business requirement to do so.

- USB ports should be blocked on all the machines. If there is a business need to use pen drives, it is highly recommended that this external media be scanned before use.

- No files should be excluded from being scanned by anti-virus software.

Note   This policy must be applied to all the computers on a network to safeguard from malicious attacks.

Business Continuity and Disaster Recovery Policy

This is one of the most important policies you'll create because it tells you how to recover quickly from service interruption or disaster, whether natural or man-made. This policy contains the set of best practices, standards, and guidelines to ensure proper risk management, which enables the company to continue to deliver products and services during a disaster.

Some of the key elements of this policy include the following:

- It's important to define what a disaster is for your organization. This can vary widely, depending on the organization and industry.

- There must be some ready-made plan for predictable disasters such as fire, earthquakes, or breakdown of products.

- Team responsibilities must be identified in order to reduce the response to the incident, which may help resolve the incident in the minimum amount of time.

- The recovery plan for the data backup and storage of the device must be defined.

Note   The organization may have a different policy for business continuity management and disaster recovery, or it could have a combined policy. This all depends on the needs and requirements of the organization.

Clear Desk and Clear Screen Policy

This policy helps reduce the risk of unauthorized access, loss, or damage of information during and outside working hours. This policy also ensures that assets containing sensitive information, such as notepads, laptops, and desktops, remain protected even when employees leave their workstations, either for a short or a long period.

Some of the important points that can be included in this policy are as follows:

- Any important business information (printed or digital) that is no longer needed must be discarded securely by using appropriate shredders.

- When you are away from your desk for a short duration, such as during lunch/tea breaks or meetings, sensitive business information should be kept in locked drawers and laptops/desktops access screens should be locked. For example, you can use Ctrl+Alt+Del or Win+L to lock Windows-based systems.

- Employees must not leave portable devices such as laptops or PDAs unattended and should physically lock these devices while away from the office.

- No loose papers should be allowed on the desks or floor.

- By default, workstations should not have access to printers.

- Automated system lockout should be enabled with information security screen savers.

Change Management Policy

The purpose of this policy is to define how changes to information security are managed and controlled, because when an organization undergoes changes in terms of business processes, tools, and technologies, the security controls may require revisions and there may be new controls to document. This policy should cover the following points:

- Define change management guidelines, including defining what a change is.

- Determine who will be responsible for verifying the change and implementing the changes.

- Manage the change record in the log sheet and change document for record purposes.

- Specify if the organization has any other SOP for managing change.

Data Retention and Disposal Policy

This policy tells you how securely the data is retained and how you dispose of data when it's no longer needed. This policy should document the lifespan of data. For example, how long is the log file data kept for record purposes.

This policy should cover the following points:

- How the data is collected and kept securely in compliance with the law and with organizational policy.

- The business should capture the minimum user data required for the business operation after getting consent from their users/employees.

- How stored data access is managed in the organization.

- An organization must have the guidelines and statutory procedures for records retention. For example:

  - The organizational records containing sensitive information that are not being used for active business should be archived until retention requirements have been met.

  - If relevant, only primary records should be archived. The duplicate records maintained elsewhere multiple times may be considered for archival.

- Similarly, organizations have guidelines for the disposal of records and data. For example:

  - When retention requirements have been met, records must be either immediately destroyed or placed in secure locations.

  - Before disposing of the data or any other assets, get the required approvals to avoid any miscommunication.

Note   This policy is intended to ensure that the information is uniformly used and disclosed by all organizational policies. A combination of physical security, personnel security, and system security mechanisms are used to achieve this standard.

Email Usage Policy

The purpose of this policy is to ensure acceptable use of email services provided by the organization to its users/employees to conduct business in an ethical, legal, and lawful manner. It should cover the following points:

- All components of the email system, including any messages created, sent, received, or stored locally on the user system or on the mail server in any form, are considered organizational property.

- The company email system should not be used under any circumstances for the creation or distribution of any disruptive or offensive messages, including ones about race, gender, hair color, disabilities, age, sexual orientation, pornography, vulgar jokes, religious beliefs and practice, and political beliefs or national origin.

- The employee should not forward any viruses or hoax email messages to company email addresses and groups that they receive through their company or personal email address. These messages must be immediately reported to the IT Helpdesk.

- The employee should not use company email to infringe on the copyright or other intellectual property rights of others.

- The employee should not distribute abusive, fraudulent, or harassing messages and avoid writing messages in any unethical, illegal, or wrongful manner.

Note   The points described here are examples only. Your company may draft other points, based on their needs and culture.

Encryption Policy

The objective of this policy is to provide direction about the use of encryption to protect information resources that contain, process, or transmit confidential and business-sensitive information. It also addresses controls over confidential data. It should cover the following:

- Technology is implemented for encrypting confidential and other sensitive data. Key length requirements for encryption should be defined.

- Confidential information stored on portable devices such as laptops must be encrypted using products and methods approved by the security officer, such as full disk encryption with pre-boot authentication.

- Portable devices, including laptops, tablets, and smartphones cannot be used for the long-term storage of any confidential information.

- Data transmission must be secure. For example, if the organization has an ecommerce site, the data must be transmitted on a secure channel.

This policy should also cover the key management procedure that an organization wants to follow. For example:

- Keys in storage and transit should be encrypted. Private keys are kept confidential.

- Keys should be randomly chosen from the entire key space, using hardware-based randomization.

Note   Under certain situations, the organization may grant or issue an exception to the use of encryption on portable computing devices and non-organization owned computing devices containing confidential data.

Information Security Policy

The purpose of the information security policy is to provide complete security from all ends and ensure the protection of the organization's information assets from all threats, whether internal or external, planned or accidental. The information security policy should cover all the software and hardware devices, the physical parameters, and its human resources.

The information security policy should cover the following points:

- Information should be made available to organizational staff and the public with minimal interruption to the business process.

- Critical information is protected from unauthorized access, use, disclosure, modification, and disposal, whether intentional or unintentional.

- The information security team must show a commitment to the continual improvement of the information security management system.

- Risk assessment and treatment is reviewed at predefined intervals. (Recommended interval is every six months.)

Incident Management Policy

This purpose of this policy is to define how the incident can be managed and reported in the organization. It should cover:

- Security Incident Management Practice Standard. For example:

  - Whenever a security incident occurs in the organization, report it to the information security team or IT team with the corrective and preventive actions.

  - Define who is responsible for initiating, completing, and documenting the incident investigation.

- Define the incident reporting flow.

- Store the incident information for learning and for future improvement purposes. You will read more about this in Chapter 10.

Information Classification Policy

The purpose of this policy is to classify the information appropriately and to ensure that the information created, treated, and stored by the organization will reach intended addressees only. It should cover the following points:

- Document classification such as internal, external, public and restricted.

- Confidential documents should be used by only a few people or departments. No one has access to confidential document other than the defined set of people.

Legal Compliance Policy

The purpose of this policy is to address the legal, statutory, regulatory, and contractual obligations arising from the security and privacy requirements of an organization. It should cover the following points:

- All relevant statutory, regulatory, and contractual requirements should be documented and kept updated by HR and the legal team.

- Relevant standards and procedures should be defined and implemented by the information security team in consultation with HR and the legal team to ensure compliance with legal/contractual obligations on the use of information with respect to intellectual property rights.

- Any guidance on essential legal requirements should be taken from management.

- If any incidents relating to legal compliance occur, define how they will be handled and managed.

Network Security and Information Transfer Policy

The purpose of this policy document is to ensure the protection of information in networks and software when they are exchanged outside the organization. It should cover the following points:

- Proper exchange of information through the electronic communication channel. Define the restricted and acceptable communication channels.

- Regulations for external parties, such as vendors and service providers for hardware and software.

- Define the security measures required to protect network services.

- Segregate the network inside the organization. For example, the public domain, IT department, and any other departments should be separated.

Password Creation Policy

The purpose of this policy is to secure password management by establishing a set a standard procedures for the creation of strong passwords, the protection of those passwords, and the frequency of change. It should include the following points:

- Define the standard guidelines for password management. For example, how long should passwords be and the combinations required to make them strong.

- Define the password change frequency. For example, some organizations require password changes every 60 to 90 days.

- Define the password protection standard clearly and communicate it to all employees.

Note   Do not share passwords with anyone, including any of the departments like HR, admin, or IT. All passwords must be treated as sensitive, confidential information.

Physical and Environmental Security Policy

The purpose of this document is to secure the organization from physical and environmental threats. It should cover the following items:

- All the organizational perimeters should be physical secured from unauthorized entry and exit.

- Identify the secure zones that have entry permitted only to authorized individuals. For example, datacenters.

- Maintain appropriate environmental conditions for employees at work, such as lighting, temperature, and hygienic conditions.

Privacy and Protection of Personally Identifiable Information Management Policy

The purpose of this policy is to establish the guidelines for protecting the confidential information belonging to users/employees/clients. Their personally identifiable information must be kept private and cannot be disclosed without their consent. It should cover the following points:

- The aspects of securing data and privacy, especially for securing personally identifiable information. For example, your name, email, address, and other personal information.

- Whenever data of personally identified information needs to be stored, it is necessary to get consent from the person/organization whose data is to be stored. It is also important to communicate the purpose of storing the data with a defined time period.

Remote Access Policy

The purpose of this policy is to define and document procedures to protect confidential data that can be compromised without this policy. A teleworking policy is meant for those people who access the computers or servers from their home or during travel. It should cover the following points:

- Two-factor authentication should be required to access the company's resources.

- This policy should define who can work remotely and connect to the organization's virtual private network (VPN).

- Authorized users must ensure that their remote access connections to the organizational LAN are treated with the same level of security.

Note   This policy applies to any person who is authorized to access a computer or device on the organization's private LAN. This includes but is not limited to contractors, temporary workers, vendors, subcontractors, employees, and attorneys authorized to access any of the organization's private LAN via remote access, for any reason.

Supplier Relationship Management Policy

The purpose of this policy is to provide guidelines to manage the supplier relationship and ensure secure supplier management activities to be carried out. It covers the following points:

- Define the information that will be accessed by the supplier and what security measures will be implemented to secure the information from unauthorized access or use. For example, signing of NDAs (non-disclosure agreements) or agreement with suppliers.

- Before engaging with the contractor or supplier, an organization must review the agreement in place.

- Define how to select and develop a relationship with suppliers and vendors that delivers the highest standards of performance and allows profitable outcomes for both parties.

Technical Vulnerabilities Management Policy

The purpose of this policy is to keep the components of the information technology infrastructure available to the organization's end users. To keep the infrastructure available all the time to users, it is important to keep the hardware, software, and services up to date with the latest patches. This policy defines and documents the procedures required for patch management. It should cover the following points:

- The IT department should maintain the inventory of all the assets and components within the organization's IT infrastructure.

- All software and hardware devices must be scanned on the network to identify any technical vulnerabilities.

- Security certificates and weaknesses need to be reviewed regularly.

- Regular VAPTs (vulnerability assessment penetration tests) must be done on the applications to ensure there are no issues.

- The roles and responsibilities of the employees must be clearly defined, including defining who is responsible for patch management and VAPT.

Note   This policy is applicable to all software development and IT teams and should discuss all the aspects to address the security vulnerability.

These policies and procedure are further explained in this chapter in the control sections. This will help you understand what these policies and procedure should cover in order to cater to the needs of the security controls as per the ISO 27001 standard.

Understanding and Implementing Controls

This section explains how to implement the security controls covered in the ISO 27001 standard. Although these security controls are somewhat self-explanatory, this section simplifies them further by including real-world examples, including what needs to be done and which documents to prepare.

The motive is to help the implementation teams complete the implementation in their areas in a smooth manner. If you implement these controls effectively, it ensures you that you are on the right path in securing the company's information. From there, it becomes the duty of each employee to maintain the security levels at all times.

The following sections explain each ISO 27001 control and give examples as well.

A.5 Information Security Policies

A.5.1 Management Direction for Information Security

Objective: To provide management direction and support for information security in accordance with business requirements and relevant laws and regulations.

Explanation: The focus is on management involvement, by giving direction to form all the required policies based on the type of organization's business and applicable laws.

A.5.1.1: Policies for Information Security (ISO 27001 Control)

A set of policies for information security should be defined, approved by management, published, and communicated to employees and relevant external parties.

Explanation: The requirement is to define all the information security policies. This policy is the driving force for implementing security controls. Once all policies are approved by management, it is important to communicate them with all employees and external stakeholders to make them aware of their responsibilities. They must abide by these policies and help in securing the organization's information.

Evidence that can be prepared: Policies lists, as mentioned previously, or as applicable to the organization's business requirements. All the policies must be reviewed/approved by the management/steering committee.

Who prepares it: The information security department will facilitate the creation of the policies by involving relevant departments i.e. Human Resources, IT/Helpdesk, etc. The organization should assess and analyze their implementation teams who will help define the policies.

For external audit: An external auditor conducting the ISO 27001 certification audit will check all the defined/approved policies. Also, define how communication takes place on the policies to employees/external stakeholders.

A.5.1.2: Review of the Policies for Information Security (ISO 27001 Control)

The information security policies should be reviewed at planned intervals or if significant changes occur to ensure their continuing suitability, adequacy, and effectiveness.

Explanation: Once policies are defined and approved, there must be a set frequency defined to review them and determine if they are still relevant or need improvements/changes. If changes are applicable, they must be done accordingly, and a revised policy approval must be received from management before releasing the changes to the employees and stakeholders.

Note   There could be many factors to consider when reviewing the policy, but the ISO 27001 standard states that the management review meeting results should be considered.

Evidence that can be prepared: All the revised policies must be reviewed at regular intervals and the revised policies must be approved by management.

Who prepares it: The information security department will facilitate with relevant departments heads to ensure their policies are reviewed on regular, defined intervals.

For external audit: An external auditor conducting the ISO 27001 certification audit will check that all the policies have been reviewed at regular intervals, as well as have been approved and communicated to employees and external stakeholders.

A.6 Organization of Information Security

A.6.1 Internal Organization

Objective: To establish a management framework to initiate and control the implementation and operation of information security within the organization.

Explanation: Before you initiate the ISO 27001 implementation in your organization, you need to build a framework to support the implementation teams.

This framework creates a clear path for the implementation team to follow. As mentioned earlier, sometimes you won't know where to start with new initiatives and won't know how to define the responsibilities of each person involved. This framework helps to address such issues.

The next section looks at the controls that are involved.

A.6.1.1: Information Security Roles and Responsibilities (ISO 27001 Control)

All information security responsibilities should be defined and allocated.

Explanation/what is required: You must define the roles and responsibilities related to information security and the policies based on the ISO 27001 implementation scope. If the responsibilities are not defined or if there is lot of ambiguity in each role, employees will not be clear about which areas they are accountable to.

Evidence that can be prepared: A roles and responsibilities document should cover the following risk-management activities:

- Information security responsibilities for each role based on company business.

- How assets are protected.

- How specific information security processes are to be carried out.

- Defined authorization levels for each role and supplier/vendor responsibilities.

Who prepares it: The human resources department and the information security team are responsible for defining and publishing the roles and responsibilities.

For external audit: An external auditor conducting ISO 27001 certification audit will check the roles and responsibilities defined for each role.

A.6.1.2: Segregation of Duties (ISO 27001 Control)

Conflicting duties and areas of responsibility should be segregated to reduce opportunities for unauthorized or unintentional modification or misuse of the organization's assets.

Explanation/what is required: The focus is to check on individuals who have dual responsibilities or are accountable for more than one role. The ISO 27001 standard covers the risk involved in such conflicting duties and areas of responsibility.

Consider this from an IT company example. Say Krishna is the business analyst team manager and is also responsible for QA/Software testing team. Such a scenario would be considered conflicting and the risk might increase that poses a threat to the integrity of the test result. Hence, to avoid such risks, segregation of duties is important. For example, Krishna should be responsible only for the business analyst team and Shiva should have responsibility for QA/Software testing team. This will help mitigate the risks.

The ISO 27001 standard recognizes that small organizations face challenges in segregating duties. In such scenarios, the focus should be more on monitoring the activities and maintaining the audit trails so that individual actions do not go undetected. That is why usage of tools/technology should be monitored in organizations who do sensitive transactions and handle confidential data. Tools help you track and maintain the audit trails, which can be used and analyzed whenever the doubt arises, or any incident occurs.

Evidence that can be prepared: The roles and responsibilities document should include clear segregation of duties and areas of responsibility. Also, controls should be implemented to monitor and detect unauthorized actions.

Who prepares it: The human resources department and the information security team will define and publish roles and responsibilities. The IT department can implement the controls in the tools/systems to monitor the activities and maintain the audit trails for future checks and verification purposes.

For external audit: An external auditor conducting the ISO 27001 certification audit will check the roles and responsibilities and ensure clear segregation of duties.

A.6.1.3: Contact with Authorities (ISO 27001 Control)

Appropriate contacts with relevant authorities should be maintained.

Explanation/what is required: The requirement is to define a procedure to contact with authorities when an information security incident occurs. This procedure should describe how authorities should be contacted and who will contact them from the organization. These authorities could be law/legal, regulatory bodies, etc.. Whenever any changes happen in acts/law or regulations, that needs to be implemented by the organization, and it must be communicated by the regulatory bodies. Hence being in contact with authorities is always useful.

When incidents or attacks happen through Internet sources, it might be required to contact cyber-law bodies or relevant bodies to investigate and take appropriate action. There are other authorities that an organization must be in contact with, such as fire departments, electricity suppliers, nearby hospitals, or any other emergency services. As these all have an impact on your organization's business or operations.

For example, if a fire or electrical incident occurs, you may need to contact such authorities, as such incidents may halt your operations (if it is related to business continuity, you will read more about it in this chapter). This impacts the company's revenue and reputation. Hence, the organization incident management procedure must describe what is to be done if any unexpected incident occurs.

Evidence that can be prepared: An incident management and escalation procedure should define the roles and responsibilities and explain what to do in such scenarios. For example, how to contact the authorities and who will contact them in case of incident.

Who prepares it: The information security team is responsible for preparing the document by involving relevant stakeholders/departments such as human resources, IT Helpdesk, Software Development, and other operations whose incidents are required to be reported to authorities.

For external audit: An external auditor conducting the ISO 27001 certification audit will check the incident management and escalation procedure. If an incident has occurred, they will check if the procedure was followed, including whether the incident form was used properly to report the incidents and what actions were taken for resolution.

A.6.1.4: Contact with Special Interest Groups (ISO 27001 Control)

Appropriate contacts with special interest groups or other specialist security forums and professional associations should be maintained.

Explanation/what is required: Although you learn many things from the ISO 27001 standard, you must also learn from other industry best practices and other relevant information that is published from time to time to improve your team's knowledge about who is responsible for implementing and monitoring controls on a regular basis. It is important to stay up to date and ready to prevent any information security attack on your systems. Hence, it is advisable to participate in security forums, seminars, and security interest groups that share relevant and new information with the teams.

Evidence that can be prepared: Association with security forums, participation in security forums and seminars, etc. can be shown as evidence.

Who prepares it: The information security team is responsible for maintaining the records of associations and participations.

For external audit: An external auditor conducting the ISO 27001 certification audit may check all the security forums or seminars that the organization is associated with and their participation.

A.6.1.5: Information Security in Project Management (ISO 27001 Control)

There must be information security in project management regardless of the type of project.

Explanation/what is required: The focus is to identify the information security risks in the project. Organizations that work on project delivery (including development, testing, facility management, and support processes) must do risk assessment exercises at the project initiation phase, as this will help identify various information security risks. This helps you prepare the mitigation plan by identifying the appropriate security controls. You must ensure that the information security risks are identified for all the phases of the project until it is delivered/closed.

Note   It's also important to regularly review risks, as this helps you analyze whether the identified security controls are reducing the threat levels or not.

Evidence that can be prepared: Create a risk-management procedure to explain how risk management is done in the projects and define the stakeholders' roles and responsibilities. Use project risk registers and trackers with identified risks and mitigation actions, i.e. security controls.

Some examples that could help in identifying information security risks are as follows:

- *Analyze the project/product requirements risks:* Most information security risks must be identified based on the requirements.

- *Access control risks:* Team members working on the project have access to project requirements and another project information. This is important as some projects are confidential, and your clients should not compromise the information security.

- *Business continuity risks:* Assess whether any business continuity aspects could impact the project, based on the customer requirements, customer geographical location, your company geographical locations, and the vendors supporting you in the project by providing the services.

- *Any legal/regulatory risks:* Assess if laws could impact your project if certain requirements based on those laws are not fulfilled. These laws could be country, regional, or state laws.

- *Contract risks:* Assess risks based on the contract terms, such as if the project is not completed on time or does not meet the quality requirements stated in the contract. What it could this pose to your project and organization?

There could be many more areas, which you can assess to minimize the information security risks. By assessing these project risks, you ensure that your organization's objectives are fulfilled by meeting the project security objectives.

Who prepares it: Using a risk register or tracker, the project managers identify risks in discussion with various project stakeholders. The information security team could be consulted to ensure that all the risks have been identified and that the controls are appropriate.

For external audit: An external auditor conducting the ISO 27001 certification audit will check the risk management procedure and project risk register, in order to check how information security risks are identified and mitigated.

A.6.2.1: Mobile Device Policy (ISO 27001 Control)

A policy and supporting security measures should be adopted to manage the risks introduced by mobile devices.

Explanation/what is required: The focus is on the use of mobile devices to access organization information that could pose information security risks. Some of the examples of mobile devices are smartphones, tablets, laptop computers, etc.

We cannot deny use of mobile device these days, as it is a fast and easy medium to access information anywhere in a fast-paced world. At the same time, these devices are vulnerable to theft, loss, hacking, and unauthorized access while you leave them unattended.

Note   Sometimes organizations allow employees to bring and use their own/
personal mobile device. In such scenarios, appropriate controls must be
implemented so that organization's information is protected on these devices.

Hence, the ISO 27001 standard guides you to be more aware and vigilant when you
use mobile devices outside the premises, as you are carrying with you the organization's
confidential information.

Evidence that can be prepared: A mobile device policy could be prepared, which
must clearly state the usage of mobile devices inside and outside the organization.
Conduct awareness sessions and maintain records about these sessions.

Note   It is important to make employees/contractors aware of how to use these
devices safely and remain vigilant of their surroundings.

The following example controls could be implemented to safely use mobile devices
(also stated in the ISO 27002-2013 code of practice). An organization can assess and
implement their controls as necessary to its business operations.

- Mobile devices given to employees/contractors must be registered.
  This helps ensure that only registered devices are using your office
  network and the information is accessed from a known device only. It
  is possible when organizations are monitoring them.

- Employees should not be allowed to install software on these
  devices on their own, as this could pose an information security risk.
  Required software must be installed by an authorized individual,
  such as a member of the IT Helpdesk team. It is advisable to disable
  installation by anyone else.

- Ensure that security patches are updated on these devices on time.
  Devices that could not be patched must be tracked and updated as
  soon as possible.

- These devices must be automatically locked out when unattended for a few minutes and must be password protected. They must use a phone screen lock password or a folder password. If they are stolen or lost, unauthorized people should not be able to gain access to these devices.

- Ensure that antivirus software is running on these devices so that a regular scan can be performed on the device to detect any virus or malware.

- Regular backups are also performed so that information can be retrieved in any unexpected incident.

- The policy must also explain what employees should do to report an incident (stolen or lost phone) to the IT Helpdesk team and to their immediate supervisors, so that they can also take steps to minimize the risk of information being accessed.

- Users should sign an end-user agreement before they get access to a mobile device. It makes them aware and reminds them of their duties to protect the information.

Who prepares it: The IT Helpdesk team, in consultation with the information security team, can define the mobile device policy. Awareness sessions can be conducted for mobile device users. Be sure to include end-user agreements for the users of mobile devices to sign.

The IT Helpdesk team will implement all the security controls, as well as any other controls that they deem important based on their experience, skills, and business needs.

For external audit: The external auditor conducting the ISO 27001 certification audit will check the mobile device policy, check how awareness sessions are conducted, and will check the required security controls. Also, if an incident occurs, they will check the steps that were planned and executed.

A.6.2.2: Teleworking (ISO 27001 Control)

A policy and supporting security measures should be implemented to protect the information accessed, processed, or stored at the teleworking sites.

Explanation/what is required: The focus is which security measures should be implemented to protect information during its access, processing, or storage at teleworking sites.

The following are example points that could be considered for an information security risk assessment when teleworking sites need to be used:

- The physical environment must be secured while accessing teleworking sites.

- When accessing organization internal systems through remote access, the information that will be accessed should be analyzed (i.e., is it confidential) and you need to know whether the communication channel is secure or not. A virtual private network (VPN) is used.

- When employees are accessing information from home, family members or friends might try to gain unauthorized access.

- When clients or external devices that are not provided by the organization access company information, it could be done via a virtual desktop access, as it would eliminate the need of processing and storage of information on such devices.

Evidence that can be prepared:

- A teleworking policy can be prepared.

- List of VPN license/accounts.

- List of current users who have VPN access.

- List of incidents and actions that were taken.

Who prepares it: The IT Helpdesk team, with the help of the information security team, creates the policy. The IT Helpdesk team also:

- Creates and maintains the list of VPN license/accounts and the list of users who have VPN access.

- Maintains the list of incidents and actions.

A.7 Human Resources Security

A.7.1 Prior to Employment

Objective: To ensure that employees and contractors understand their responsibilities and are suited to the roles for which they are considered.

Explanation: Before new employees and contractors get access to company information and assets, it becomes an important duty of the organization to make them aware of their work-related responsibilities and the safety measures they need to follow. It also is important that people are assigned to the right roles in terms of having the relevant skills, experience, and education.

The goal is to prevent employees or contractors from stealing company information or assets or sharing them with competitors for personal gain. The following sections cover the controls that fall under human resources-related security.

A.7.1.1: Screening (ISO 27001 Control)

Carry out background verification on all candidates for employment in accordance with relevant laws, regulations, and ethics. These checks should be proportional to the business requirements, the classification of the information to be accessed, and the perceived risks.

Explanation/what is required: This control requires the organization to perform background checks on all people who will work for the company. This ensures that potential candidates don't have fake identities or a serious criminal background that could pose as a risk to the organization, its customers, or fellow employees. The human resources department can perform these checks. Some companies outsource the background verification responsibility to experts or agencies.

The company must collect evidence about the candidate, such as educational certificates, the previous company where they worked, whether the company exists, and so on. This can be checked by verifying the company's website and contacting their human resources team. You can also call the person's references. All this will help in assessing the risk associated with the candidate and whether they can be hired.

Evidence that can be prepared: Background checks and reports on each candidate.

What is included in this report: Candidate names, the date on which the verification check was performed, the names and contact details of the people who were contacted, and the feedback noted about the candidate. Educational and criminal checks should also be documented.

During their first ISO 27001 implementation, some organizations might not conduct criminal checks on the candidates, so they must mention this in their standard operating procedure and note it as a risk in the human resources department risk assessment tracker.

Who prepares it: The human resources department or the outsource vendor hired for background checks.

For external audit: The external auditor conducting the ISO 27001 certification audit will check for background checks of the employees joined in the past six or three months, depending on the implementation period in the organization. Figure 6-1 shows the front page of the background verification form. The complete template can be downloaded from the resources section of this book.

Employment Verification Form – \<Company Name\>

Applicant No/ Employee ID	Work Location	Date of Joining/Interview

Please provide complete and correct information. All fields are mandatory.
Please do not use short forms / abbreviations.

Personal Details	
Full Name (First, Middle, Last)	
Date of Birth (dd/mm/yy)	Gender: ☐ Male ☐ Female
Father's Name:	Mobile Number:
Permanent Address with Landmark:	
NSR (National Skills Registry) Number if any:	
Nationality:	

Figure 6-1. *Front page of a background verification form*

A.7.1.2 Terms and Conditions of Employment (ISO 27001 Control)

The contractual agreements with employees and contractors should state their and the organization's responsibilities for information security.

Explanation/what is required: This control requires the company to define the terms and conditions of the employment contract. This should clearly state security responsibilities to be adhered by employees and contractors during their employment.

The goal is to make employees aware of these terms. Companies can take action as per the law if company information or assets are misused.

Evidence that can be prepared: A signed employment contract or offer letter (covering terms and conditions).

Who prepares it: The human resources department maintains signed hard copies of the employment contract or offer letter. Scanned soft copies could be maintained as a backup.

For external audit: The external auditor conducting the ISO 27001 certification audit will check for a signed employment contract or offer letter. Also, they will check whether all the terms and conditions are stated clearly and completely.

A.7.2 During Employment

Objective: To ensure that employees and contractors are aware of and fulfill their information security responsibilities.

Explanation: Employees are fully aware of the threats to their data that occur during their daily job activities and understand their responsibilities to mitigate these threats.

A.7.2.1 Management Responsibilities (ISO 27001 Control)

Management should require all employees and contractors to follow the information security guidelines in accordance with the established policies and procedures of the organization.

Explanation/what is required: This control requires management to communicate to employees and contractors the standard operating procedures to ensure that security practices are implemented accordingly.

Evidence that can be prepared: Communication emails, minutes of the meeting, and signed/approved policies and procedures.

Who prepares it: An email from management, and the minutes of a meeting to be maintained by the information security team. The information security department should also maintain signed hard copies of approved policies and procedures and scan soft copies to be maintained as a backup.

For external audit: The external auditor conducting the ISO 27001 certification audit will check for the evidence.

A.7.2.2 Information Security Awareness, Education, and Training (ISO 27001 Control)

All employees of the organization and, when relevant, contractors should receive appropriate awareness training and regular updates to organizational policies and procedures, as relevant to their job function.

Explanation/what is required: Information security awareness sessions should be planned and conducted for all the employees, including your support staff, such as cleaners, security guards, etc. Whenever any changes/updates take place to any of the policies or standard operating procedures, employees must be made aware of them. These awareness sessions must be conducted for contractors and third-party users as well, as they also pose risks to information security.

Awareness helps reduce security risks, so these awareness sessions must be conducted on a regular basis and should be a mandatory part of the new hire induction program.

Evidence that can be prepared: Attendance records of participants/employees who attended the awareness sessions. Feedback forms and records of any quizzes.

Who prepares it: Awareness sessions are conducted by the information security department. Whenever sessions are conducted, attendance records need to be maintained.

For external audit: The external auditor conducting the ISO 27001 certification audit will check for the records of the awareness sessions. The auditor can ask questions randomly to any employee to check their knowledge.

A.7.2.3 Disciplinary Process (ISO 27001 Control)

There should be a formal and communicated disciplinary process in place to take action against employees who have committed an information security breach.

Explanation/what is required: There must be a defined policy or a standard operating procedure that covers the disciplinary steps to be taken in the case of misconduct

Evidence that can be prepared: Disciplinary policy or a standard operating procedure, or both, could be prepared. Feedback forms.

Who prepares it: The human resources department.

For external audit: The external auditor conducting the ISO 27001 certification audit will check for the disciplinary policy or a standard operating procedure.

A.7.3 Termination or Change of Employment

Objective: To protect the organization's interests as part of the process of changing or terminating employment.

Explanation: Whenever any employee and contractor exits the organization their exit formalities must be done systematically. Also, within the organization, if there is a change in employment responsibilities, there should also be a standard process.

A.7.3.1 Termination or Change of Employment Responsibilities (ISO 27001 Control)

Information security responsibilities and duties that remain valid after termination or change of employment should be defined and communicated to the employee or contractor and enforced.

Explanation/what is required: The focus here is on the following things:

- When an employee/contractor joins and then leaves the company/ organization.

- An employee could transfer from one location to another within the organization.

- Employee/contractor responsibilities can change, i.e., they could be increased or decreased.

When employees leave The organization must define a clear policy or standard operating procedure that explains when employees/contractors leave the organization, what they must do to complete all the exit formalities. This is to ensure that the exit is done in a safe manner without any impact to organizational information.

It is important to ensure that exiting employees/contractors do not have access to sensitive information or assets after their last day.

Clients also know the importance of safeguarding their information, and they could also communicate their own standard operating procedures to you to follow when an employee/contractor working for your client leaves. It is the duty of the organization to ensure that exiting employees abide by these defined policies.

When employees transfer to another department Employees could move from one office location to another office or department. Say that employee Krishna is working at office location A and then is transferred to office location B. It becomes important for the organization to review and revoke Krishna's access from the information, assets, tools/applications, etc. that are relevant only to location A and to ensure that he has access to location B's data and information only.

Even when the employee transfers from one department to another, you must follow the same process and review/revoke access accordingly.

The responsibilities of an employee change Employee or contractor responsibilities could undergo changes, for example, they might get additional/new responsibilities and maybe old responsibilities become no longer valid. In such scenarios, it's important to review/revoke the access accordingly.

Evidence that can be prepared: The human resources (HR) department typically manages employee exits and transfers, so HR should define the policy that covers these scenarios and should ensure that this information is communicated to employees and contractors.

The evidence can be an employee exit form on which every department lists the information for which access needs to be revoked and assets to be returned. On their last day, the employee must return all the assets issued by every department. Every department head must sign the employee exit form to confirm that the employee has returned all assets. Once the employee exit form has been signed by every department head, then the HR department should relieve the employee by providing a company relieving certificate or an experience certificate (as per the human resources norms/standards).

Note   Organizations that do not use a paper-based approach for the employee exit form can use ticket-based tools or email communication. It is up to the organization to decide which method is effective and useful. In any case, evidentiary records need to be maintained for a longer period and should be easily available for audit/verification purposes.

IT companies and IT departments in any organization must ensure that the user ID of the employee/contractor is disabled in the system on the last day (the record must be available in the system for audit purposes) to ensure no tools or applications are accessible.

An example exit clearance form is shown in Figure 6-2, for reference. The complete form can be downloaded from the book's resources.

Employee Exit Clearance Form					
SECTION I.					
Employee Nam				**Last Date Of Working :**	
Emp ID Number:				**Department**	
Emp Forwarding Mail Address:				**Contact Number**	
SECTION II.					
Departments / Representative	**Clearance Item**	**Status - Yes, No, NA**	**Provide Remarks (When status is No &/or action is required)**	**Signature of Responsible Department Representative with date**	
Supervisor / Reporting Manager	(1) Collect final time-sheet from employee ensuring that all personal/sick leave has been recorded.				
	(2) Documents - relevant/important documents in soft/hard manner collected prepared by the employee				
	(3) Knowledge Transfer excercise is complete				

Figure 6-2. *Employee exit clearance form*

A.8 Asset Management

A.8.1 Responsibility for Assets

Objective: To identify organizational assets and define appropriate protection responsibilities.

Explanation: The objective is to identify all the assets associated with the organization and then define security controls needed to safeguard those assets.

The next sections explain the controls in asset management.

A.8.1.1 Inventory of Assets (ISO 27001 Control)

Assets associated with information and information processing facilities should be identified and an inventory of these assets should be drawn up and maintained.

Explanation/what is required: The first step is to create an asset list by identifying the relevant assets. An inventory of these assets needs to be managed throughout their lifecycle, which includes creation, processing, storage, transmission, deletion, and destruction.

Note   The inventory of your assets should be accurate and up to date in order to best manage organizational risk.

Evidence that can be prepared: An asset register should be prepared.

Who prepares it: The relevant department head/team members should prepare the asset register. For example, an HR asset inventory should be prepared by HR and the IT assets inventory should be prepared by the IT team/department.

For external audit: An external auditor may check for an asset register during the ISO 27001 audit.

A.8.1.2 Ownership of Assets (ISO 27001 Control)

Assets maintained in the inventory should be owned.

Explanation/what is required: This control requires you to have assigned an owner to every asset. Whenever new assets are created or transferred to the organization, you should define who will be responsible for the management of that asset throughout the lifecycle. The asset owner is responsible for:

- Ensuring that the asset register is correct and up to date.

- Ensuring that assets are classified into appropriate categories and protected.

- Defining the asset management policy and reviewing it periodically.

- Properly handling assets while deleting or destroying them.

Evidence that can be prepared: Asset management policy and an asset register.

Who prepares it: The information security team should prepare the asset management policy and the relevant asset owner/department should prepare the asset register.

For external audit: An external auditor may check for this evidence, to verify that asset management practices are followed and managed throughout the asset's lifecycle.

A.8.1.3 Acceptable Use of Assets (ISO 27001 Control)

Rules for the acceptable use of information and assets associated with information and information processing facilities should be identified, documented, and implemented.

Explanation: Assets are used by the organization and their suppliers or vendors and they must understand the information security requirement associated with each asset. Hence, they should be responsible for the assets provided to them for official use.

Evidence that can be prepared: Acceptable usages policy.

Who prepares it: The information security team and the relevant asset owner/ department prepares the acceptable usages policies.

For external audit: An external auditor may check for the acceptable usages policy during the ISO 27001 audit.

A.8.1.4 Return of Assets (Control ISO 27001)

All employees and external party users should return all the organizational assets in their possession upon termination of their employment, contract, or agreement.

Explanation/what is required: This control explains the return of assets. For example, the employee or the vendor must return all the organizational assets when their project, contract, or agreement is closed. Upon termination of employment, assets such as laptops, company IDs, or any other asset provided by the company must be returned.

If an employee or external party is leaving the organization, they must document any job knowledge that is required for the smooth operation of the company. This document is sometimes known as knowledge transfer (KT)

Evidence that can be prepared: The exit form should indicate whether all assets have been returned.

Who prepares it: Each department head is responsible for collecting their assets and keeping records of that process.

For external audit: An external auditor may check for evidence in the form of physical or soft copies of reports or documents.

Note   The organization should watch for unauthorized copying of information, especially after notice of termination, to ensure that no intellectual property or copyrights are violated.

A.8.2 Information Classification

Objective: To ensure that information receives an appropriate level of protection in accordance with its importance to the organization.

Explanation: This control helps classify information, which is very important for the organization. All information is not critical and at the same time, all information cannot be shared with the public. Hence, the classification of information plays an important role. The next sections discuss the controls related to information classification.

A.8.2.1 Classification of Information (Control ISO 27001)

Information should be classified in terms of legal requirements, value, criticality, and sensitivity to unauthorized disclosure or modification.

Explanation/what is required: The control says that classification of information should be done based on criticality, value, and sensitivity. The information classification should be done based on a risk assessment activity. Information classification must be defined based on the business need and there must be a process for defining and documenting information classification.

The frequency of information classification should be defined in the policy and should be updated based on the value and criticality of the information.

Evidence that can be prepared: Information classification policy and information classification guideline.

Who prepares it: The Information security team is responsible for preparing the information classification policy and guideline.

For external audit: The external auditor in the ISO 27001 audit will check for this document.

A.8.2.2 Labeling of Information (Control ISO 27001)

An appropriate set of procedures for information labeling should be developed and implemented in accordance with the information classification scheme adopted by the organization.

Explanation/what is required: This control covers the procedures required for labeling information assets under the classification plan of the organization. You need to mention:

- Where and how the label can be attached

- On what types of media labeling is required

- Where labeling is not required

Evidence that can be prepared: Information classification policy and information classification guideline.

Who prepares it: The information security team is responsible for preparing the information classification policy and guideline.

For external audit: The auditor will look at the records for information labeling along with the policy document.

A.8.2.3 Handling of Assets (Control ISO 27001)

Procedures for handling assets should be developed and implemented in accordance with the information classification scheme adopted by the organization.

Explanation/what is required: This control ensures the proper handling of assets by having a clear procedure for processing, storing, and communicating information assets. These steps required to ensure secure handling of assets:

- Maintain a record for use by authorized recipients.

- Implement access restrictions for each level of information classification.

- Store the IT assets as per the manufacturer instructions only.

Note   An agreement should be in place when the assets are used by other organizations/external parties on a sharing basis.

Evidence that can be prepared: Asset tracker and procedures for asset handling.

Who prepares it: Asset owners are responsible for handling assets and the information security team will facilitate with the asset handling procedure by getting input from various departments.

For external audit: The auditor will look at the records for asset handling along with the policy document.

A.8.3 Media Handling

Objective: To prevent unauthorized disclosure, modification, removal, or destruction of information stored on media.

Explanation: The objective is to prevent any kind of unauthorized access on a media device. This includes how you manage of media, how to dispose of media securely, and the physical media transfer. The next sections cover all the controls.

A.8.3.1 Management of Removable Media (Control ISO 27001)

Procedures should be implemented for the removable of media in accordance with the classification scheme adopted by the organization.

Explanation/what is required: This control focuses on the management of removable media. The procedure should be defined to protect and manage removable media. The following points should be considered:

- All the removable media should be stored in a safe and secure environment.

- To reduce the risk of data damage, there should be multiple media devices to store business-critical data/information.

- Confidential information should be protected with a cryptographic technique.

- Restrict the use of external drives such as hard disks, stick devices, etc.

Evidence that can be prepared: Prepare the procedure for the management of removable devices.

Who prepares it: The IT team is responsible for records related to media transfer. Policies should also be defined and implemented with the support of the information security team.

For external audit: The external auditor will look for this document.

Note   Some external auditors may also physically check whether the removable device is blocked as per the policy document to confirm the compliance.

A.8.3.2 Disposal of Media (Control ISO 27001)

Media should be disposed of securely when it's no longer required, using formal procedures.

Explanation/what is required: This control covers media disposal. For example, if you have information that is 10 years old and stored on media that is no longer needed, you need a policy to remove that data. This can all be part of your media disposal policy. For the implementation of this control, the following points should be considered:

- Media that contains confidential information should be removed securely. For example, you may use shredders to destroy the information or any other tool.

- Write a procedure for identifying and securely disposing of media containing sensitive information.

- Maintain an audit trail for secure disposable of such media.

Evidence that can be prepared: The procedure document can be prepared to explain how you securely dispose of the media.

Who prepares it: The disposal of media is the responsibility of the IT departments and they must also prepare the procedure for securing media disposal with the help of the information security team.

For external audit: The external auditor will look for media disposal policy and procedure. They may ask for the media disposal records.

A.8.3.3 Physical Media Transfer (Control ISO 27001)

Media containing valuable information should be protected against unauthorized access, misuse, or corruption during transportation.

Explanation/what is required: This control covers securing physical media transfer. Consider these points to implement this control:

- Identify the list of courier services and choose a reliable partner.

- Protect the content by using a quality package that restricts the courier from seeing the content and reducing the chances of physical damage.

Evidence that can be prepared: A tracking log can be maintained to track media transfer. Tracking slips can be kept for record purposes.

Who prepares it: The admin from the IT team and the facility team should be responsible for creating the procedure and keeping the records in place.

For external audit: The external auditor may ask for the records and processes used to secure physical media transfer.

Note   After selecting a reliable courier partner, there must be an agreement between both the partners.

A.9 Access Control

A.9.1 Business Requirements of access Control

Objective: To limit access to information and information processing facilities.

Explanation/what is required: The objective is to protect information security by limiting the access to company information, systems, and tools. Limiting the access means providing access controls only up at required levels, as loose access may increase the risk of an information security breach.

A.9.1.1 Access Control Policy (ISO 27001 Control)

As access control policy should be established, documented, and reviewed based on the business and information security requirements.

Explanation/what is required: The requirement is to design a policy for managing access rights permissions to information and various assets of the organization. It is important that access controls rights are specific to each user role.

To design an access control policy, organizations should consider the following points, mapping them with their business requirements:

- Assess your business application security requirements.

- Access rights are based on the information classification guidelines.

- Assess the relevant laws and contractual requirements before allotting access rights.

- Determine how access to the information will be requested, authorized, and administered.

- Determine how privileged access rights will be allotted and managed.

- Determine how access rights will be reviewed at regular intervals.

- Determine how removal of access rights will be requested and managed.

Evidence that can be prepared: Access control policy and risk tracker (with identified risks as part of access permissions).

Who prepares it: Information security needs to get input from various departments including critical ones, such as the IT Helpdesk team, to define access control policy.

For external audit: An external auditor conducting the ISO 27001 certification audit will check the access control policy in order to verify how the organization has defined and communicated the policy to all stakeholders.

A.9.1.2 Access to Networks and Network Services (ISO 27001 Control)

Users should only be provided access to the network and network services that they have been specifically authorized to use.

Explanation/what is required: The requirement is the same as the objective says, organizations must ensure only authorized users/employees are provided access to organization network and network services. Any unauthorized use can pose a threat to the organization's information.

The network policy should cover the following:

- Information on networks that is accessible

- How the users/employees would be authenticated for permissions

- Mode of using the network i.e. wireless, LAN, VPN, etc.

- How network will be monitored to safeguard information

Evidence that can be prepared: Access control policy, network control policy, network diagram, and network monitoring logs

Who prepares it: The IT Helpdesk team along with the information security team would prepare the evidence.

For external audit: An external auditor conducting the ISO 27001 certification audit will check the evidence in order to verify how the organization has defined and implemented network policy, measures taken to protect network and network services.

A.9.2 User Access Management

Objective: To ensure authorized user access and to prevent unauthorized access to systems and services.

Explanation/what is required: Protect information security by ensuring only authorized users gain access to organization system and services. Also, implement security controls to prevent access to any unauthorized users.

A.9.2.1 User Registration and De-Registration (ISO 27001 Control)

A formal user registration and de-registration process should be implemented to enable assignment of access rights.

Explanation/what is required: The requirement is to design a procedure that should cover how a user registration and de-registration will be done in different scenarios. The following points could be covered, based on organizational needs:

- Every user must be allotted a unique ID, so it's easy to identify the user and track him. If a security breach takes place, the user/employee will be held responsible and disciplinary action will be taken.

- Ensure that there are no shared IDs used. In scenarios where it is required for business purposes, it must be approved by authority members, and documented and monitored on a regular basis. Shared user IDs are usually risk prone as when security breach happens, it is sometimes difficult to assess who was responsible because the same user ID is used by several users.

- Once an employee leaves the organization, his/her user ID must be disabled immediately to avoid any information security breach.

- Ensure that there is a periodic review performed on user IDs to identify whether any redundant user IDs exist. They should immediately be disabled.

- Determine how requests will be made for assigning and revoking user IDs. It must be clear who can raise the request, approvals required, etc.

Evidence that can be prepared: Access control policy, user registration/de-registration procedures, requests raised for user registration/de-registration, evidence for user registration and disabling of user IDs, list of active and disabled user IDs, and monitoring records of user IDs at regular intervals

Who prepares it: The IT Helpdesk team along with the information security team would prepare the evidence.

For external audit: An external auditor conducting the ISO 27001 certification audit will check the evidence in order to verify how the organization has defined and implemented user registration and de-registration procedure. They might also check when user/employees left the organization and see Whether user IDs are disabled immediately or not.

A.9.2.2 User access provisioning (ISO 27001 Control)

A formal user access provisioning process should be implemented to assign or revoke access rights for all user types to all systems and services.

Explanation/what is required: The following points could be covered, based on organization business needs.

Before providing user access to the organization system and services, appropriate approvals must be taken from the owner of those system and services. It must be ensured that access rights are granted as per the defined policy and the roles defined for each user/designation. IDs of users whose roles have changed or have left the organization must be disabled immediately. Maintain the list of active and disabled user IDs.

Evidence that can be prepared: Access control policy, requests raised for the users for granting/revoking access, evidence for granting/revoking access for the users, list of active and disabled user IDs, monitoring records of user IDs at regular intervals

Who prepares it: The IT Helpdesk team along with the information security team would prepare the evidence.

For external audit: An external auditor conducting the ISO 27001 certification audit will check the evidence in order to verify how the organization has granted and revoked access to the users for specific information systems and services.

A.9.2.3 Management of Privileged Access Rights (ISO 27001 Control)

The allocation and use of privileged access rights should be restricted and controlled.

Explanation/what is required: Privileged access rights management is important as users with such access can modify/delete information. The following points could be covered, based on the organization's business needs:

- Identify all systems and services for which privileged user IDs are needed and users who could be provided with such IDs.

- Authorization steps and records of all privileged user IDs must be maintained.

- Expiry dates of all privileged user IDs must be defined.

- Privileged user IDs must be created separately as a unique ID, and they should not be merged with the regular user ID allotted to the users.

- For administrator user IDs, their secret authentication information must be protected, such as by change of passwords. When the user leaves the organization their user IDs must be disabled immediately.

Evidence that can be prepared: Privileged user access control policy, requests raised for the privileged users ID, evidence for granting/revoking access for the privileged users ID, list of active and disabled privileged users ID, and monitoring records of privileged users ID at regular intervals

Who prepares it: The IT Helpdesk team along with the information security team would prepare the evidence.

For external audit: An external auditor conducting the ISO 27001 certification audit will check the evidence in order to verify how the organization has managed privileged user IDs access permission rights.

A.9.2.4 Management of Secret Authentication Information of Users (ISO 27001 Control)

The allocation of secret authentication information should be controlled through a formal management process.

Explanation/what is required: Secret authentication information management is important. The following points could be covered, based on the organization's business needs:

- Users must sign a statement to secure their secret authentication information (i.e. passwords), as they are confidential information that belongs to a specific user. Sharing passwords with unauthorized users intentionally or unintentionally is an information security breach, which may pose a threat to the information.

- When secret authentication information is shared with the user, initially it must be the temporary and users must be forced to change the temporary password with something of their own secret authentication.

- Temporary secret authentication must be shared in a secure manner, to ensure that it reaches the right recipient/user only. Users must acknowledge the receipt of secret authentication information.

Evidence that can be prepared: Password control policy, procedure how secret authentication information will be created, shared, and maintained

Who prepares it: The IT Helpdesk team along with the information security team would prepare the evidence.

For external audit: An external auditor conducting the ISO 27001 certification audit will check the evidence in order to verify how the organization will create, share, and maintain secret authentication information for employees/contractors.

A.9.2.5 Review of Users Access Rights (ISO 27001 Control)

Asset owners should review users access rights at regular intervals.

Explanation/what is required: Review of user access rights is important to avoid any unauthorized access to the information/assets. The following points could be covered, based on the organization's business needs:

- Users' access rights must be reviewed at regular intervals including when users are promoted, or their roles are changed, or they leave the organization.

- Privileged user IDs must be reviewed on a more frequent basis, as such users can alter, modify, or delete information more easily than any normal users.

- Logs of privileged user IDs must be maintained whenever there are changes to the access permission rights.

Evidence that can be prepared: Password control policy, review of user access rights permissions, logs of privileged user IDs access changes, and list of disable privileged user IDs

Who prepares it: The IT Helpdesk team along with the information security team would prepare the evidence.

For external audit: An external auditor conducting the ISO 27001 certification audit will check the evidence in order to verify how the organization will review the user access rights permissions at regular intervals to avoid any security breaches.

A.9.2.6 Removal or Adjustment of Access Rights (ISO 27001 Control)

The access rights of all employees and external users to information and information processing facilities should be removed upon termination of their employment, contract, or agreement or adjusted upon change.

Explanation/what is required: The following points could be covered, based on the organization's business needs:

- The organization must ensure that access rights of employees/contractors are revoked once they leave the organization. Also, when any changes have been done in the employment (i.e. changes in the roles due to the business purposes or changes in the contract/agreement), then review of access rights must be conducted to check whether existing access rights need to be changed. These access rights could be for the authorization levels to systems/applications, identification cards, etc. For more information, refer to earlier chapters in this book.

- If the user was allotted any asset, it must be removed or submitted to the specific department before termination or employment changes.

- Known passwords for user IDs must be disabled on the last working day of the employee/contractor.

Evidence that can be prepared: Access control policy, disable requests for the user IDs/password , and list of disable user IDs/password

Who prepares it: the Human resources team raises the disable requests for the user IDs/password with the IT Helpdesk team, who will disable and maintain appropriate record/evidence. The information security team will review and provide consulting about the process.

For external audit: An external auditor conducting the ISO 27001 certification audit will check the evidence in order to verify how the organization will review and disable user IDs/passwords of users.

A.9.3 User Responsibilities

Objective: To make users accountable for safeguarding their authentication information.

Explanation/what is required: Users must protect secret authentication information shared with them for official use.

A.9.3.1 Use of Secret Authentication Information (ISO 27001 Control)

User should be required to follow the organization's practices when using secret authentication information.

Explanation/what is required: Secret authentication information shared with the user/employee must be kept confidential. It is advisable not to keep secret authentication information in written form, i.e. on paper. If password vaults are used then it can be stored, as they are more secure.

It is advisable to change secret authentication information, when there is an indication that it has been compromised. In such scenarios it must be changed immediately.

Evidence that can be prepared: Access control policy, secret authentication information policy, requests for the secret authentication information, list of users with secret authentication

Who prepares it: The IT Helpdesk team will share the secret authentication information and will maintain associated record/evidence. The information security team would review and provide consulting about the process.

For external audit: An external auditor conducting the ISO 27001 certification audit will check the evidence in order to verify how the organization will share secret authentication information with the user/employee and how it will be protected by user/employee while using it for the official purposes.

A.9.4 System and Application Access Control

Objective: To prevent unauthorized access to systems and applications.

Explanation/what is required: The objective is that organization must create provisions to prevent systems and applications from unauthorized access.

A.9.4.1 Information access restriction (ISO 27001 Control)

Access to information and application system functions should be restricted in accordance with the access control policy.

Explanation/what is required: The organization should consider the following example points, while providing access permissions to users/employees on information and application systems. As the organization provides or stores most of the information/data on application systems, restriction to access must be done in accordance with the access control policy.

- Identify the users who will access certain information/data

- Determine how the access controls will be managed for the users (i.e., read, write, and delete)

- Determine how the access rights will be managed for other applications

Evidence that can be prepared: Access control policy, list of users with access permission rights i.e. read, write, and delete for all applications, and list of active and disabled users.

Who prepares it: The IT Helpdesk team will prepare and maintain record/evidence. The information security team would review and provide consulting on the process.

For external audit: An external auditor conducting the ISO 27001 certification audit will check the evidence in order to verify how the organization will manage users with access permission rights (i.e. read, write, and delete) for all applications' data/information.

A.9.4.2 Secure Log-On Procedures (ISO 27001 Control)

Where required by the access control policy, access to systems and applications should be controlled by a secure log-on procedure.

Explanation/what is required: The organization must create provisions for secure log on procedure to get access to systems and applications. It is to confirm the identity of the valid user and provide them authorized access as per the access control policy. The organization can consider the following points for secure logon procedures:

- Users/employees are allowed inside the system only after successful completion of the secure log-on procedure.

- The organization can implement the security control by configuring a system setting that displays a warning message, that the system/computer must be used by authorized users only.

- Once all input data is entered correctly then only log-on information is validated.

- Log all the successful and unsuccessful attempts made.

- Security incidents must be logged if a security breach is observed while logged on.

- While entering the password, it should not be visible.

- Terminate the inactive session after a certain period to minimize the risk of unauthorized access.

Evidence that can be prepared: Access control policy, secure log on procedure, and list of secure log-on incidents

Who prepares it: The IT Helpdesk team will prepare and maintain record/evidence. The information security team would review and provide consulting on the process.

For external audit: An external auditor conducting the ISO 27001 certification audit will check the evidence in order to verify how the organization is managing secure log-on procedure to ensure only valid authorized users gain access to the systems.

A.9.4.3 Password Management System (ISO 27001 Control)

Password management systems should be interactive and should ensure quality passwords.

Explanation/what is required: The organization can consider the following points for password management system:

- Ensure that user ID/passwords are unique, to make the user accountable.

- Passwords must be changed at first log-on attempt, as first passwords are default passwords that must be changed by the user on their own.

- Passwords must be changed at regular intervals, such as every 60 to 90 days.

- Password logs must be maintained and previous passwords are not allowed for reuse.

- When entering the password, it should not be visible.

Evidence that can be prepared: Password creation policy, list of unique passwords per user ID, list of previous used passwords, configure system setting to change passwords every 90 days

Who prepares it: The IT Helpdesk team will prepare and maintain record/evidence. The information security team would review and provide consulting on the process.

For external audit: An external auditor conducting the ISO 27001 certification audit will check the evidence in order to verify how the organization will manage password management system to ensure no unauthorized access attempts are made.

A.9.4.4 Use of Privileged Utility Programs (ISO 27001 Control)

The use of utility programs that might be capable of overriding system and application controls should be restricted and tightly controlled.

Explanation/what is required: The organization must implement security controls to prevent utility programs from overriding the system on its own.

The following points for utility programs can be considered:

- Define the authorization levels for the utility programs

- Limit the use of utility programs

- Maintain the log information of the utility program usage

- Identify and disable all unnecessary utility programs

Evidence that can be prepared: List of utility programs in use, log information of the utility program, and list of disabled utility programs

Who prepares it: The IT Helpdesk team will prepare and maintain record/evidence. The information security team would review and provide consulting on the process.

For external audit: An external auditor conducting the ISO 27001 certification audit will check the evidence in order to verify how the organization will manage the usage of utility programs and preventing them from overriding the systems on their own.

A.9.4.5 Access Control to Program Source Code (ISO 27001 Control)

Access to program source code should be restricted.

Explanation/what is required: Organizations must implement security controls to restrict the access to program source code, to prevent unauthorized or unintentional changes to the source code. Organizations must assess the storage location of the source code, to manage the access in a better way.

Consider the following points for restricting the access to program source code:

- Persons should not have unrestricted access to the code

- Only authorized users must be allowed to update program source libraries

- Audit log must be maintained of all successful and unsuccessful access attempts to the program source libraries

- Program source code should be prohibited from copying

Evidence that can be prepared: List of authorized users access to program source code, audit log of all successful and unsuccessful access attempts to the program source libraries, and list of users with disabled access (who left organization or change in their roles)

Who prepares it: The IT Helpdesk team will prepare and maintain record/evidence. The information security team would review and provide consulting on the process.

For external audit: An external auditor conducting the ISO 27001 certification audit will check the evidence in order to verify how the organization will restrict the access to program source code to prevent the unauthorized access, unintentional changes, and source code from being copied.

A.10 Cryptography

A.10.1 Cryptographic Controls

Objective: The objective of this control is to ensure proper and effective use of cryptography to protect the confidentiality, authenticity, and/or integrity of information.

Explanation: Today we all must deal with lots of information through different mediums such as emails, online transactions, hard drives, and through other mediums. Also, the organizational information sometimes travels through different channels like ISPs, routers, switches, and via other channels before it reaches to us and thus the security of information is critical to the business. This control is divided into two parts.

A.10.1.1 Policy on the Use of Cryptographic Controls (ISO 27001 Control)

A policy on the use of cryptographic controls for protection of information should be developed and implemented.

Explanation: Define policies for cryptographic control. Cryptographic controls are implemented to provide additional safeguards against the compromise of data transmission across the public network. This control addresses encryption policy and controls for organization confidential data that is at rest (including portable devices and removable media), data in motion (transmission security), and encryption key standards and management.

Sometimes people get confused between cryptography and encryption. *Cryptography* is a science of writing in codes while *encryption* is the mechanism to convert the information in code that those who know the mechanism of encryption/decryption can understand.

Talking in code language is not new. In the old days, it was used by military leaders and diplomats to secure their information.

An example of classic cryptography: *Hello World* can be *'ehlol owrdl'*, the letters are just mixed up. In a substitution cipher, the word is replaced by different letters or group of letters. In modern cryptography, we have a wide range of techniques to secure information. However, it is such a vast field and not in the scope of this book.

Here are some real-life examples where cryptographic control can be used or implemented in your organization based on need.

- You can encrypt the devices that carry confidential information such as external hard drives and flash drives if they go outside the organization.

- If any employee travels frequently with a laptop, it must be encrypted. Use reliable free encryption software tools such as Bitlocker, Veracrypt, 7-zip, etc.

- Any email with confidential information must be secured.

- When your employees connect to the office network from home, the connection must be secured using a virtual private network (VPN).

- If you have any web portal or product that offers ecommerce services and have payment methods, the gateway must be secured.

- Any shared folder or files that are accessible by all the employees in the organization must be secured.

- USB sticks are very small devices and can be risky if the organization has no policy on their use. USB sticks must be blocked on all the devices expect a few devices with permission and known risk.

Evidence that can be prepared: A policy on the use of encryption can be prepared to identify the areas where encryption technique must be used and to define and implement the standards.

Who prepares it: The information security team is responsible for defining and implementing the encryption policy along with the IT team.

For external audit: The external auditor will check for this document during the ISO 27001 certification audit.

A.10.1.2 Key Management (ISO 27001 Control)

Control: A policy on the use, protection, and lifetime of cryptographic keys should be developed and implemented through their whole lifecycle.

Explanation: This control explains the use of policy and protection of cryptographic keys. The important aspect is about the management of keys throughout the lifecycle. It defines how you manage keys and how they are distributed, changed, and stored in the backup. Key management must be strong and safe so that the attacker cannot misuse the keys.

Here are some implementation tips:

- The information security team must verify backup storage for key passwords, files, and related backup configuration data to avoid the single point of failure and ensure access to encrypted data.

- No single individual should be authorized to generate a new key pair.

- The keys in storage and transit must be encrypted. Private keys will be kept confidential. Keys will be randomly chosen from the entire key space, using hardware-based randomization.

- The lifespan of the key should be kept short with defined activation and deactivation duration limits.

- A key-generating tool should be physically and logically secure from installation, operation, and removal of service.

Evidence that can be prepared: The policy on encryption, records-securely storage of encryption/decryption keys.

Who prepares it: The information security team is responsible for defining and implementing the encryption policy along with the IT team.

For external audit: The external auditor conducting the ISO 27001 audit may check for encryption policy and ask about the key management policy.

A.11 Physical and Environmental Security

Objective: To prevent unauthorized physical access, damage, and interference to the organization's information and information processing facilities.

Explanation: The objective in this control is to restrict illegal physical and environmental access, the term physical and environmental refers to steps taken to protect the physical system and infrastructure against physical and environmental threats. In today's world, the information around the organization is very critical. This control is broken into two parts A.11.1, "Secure Areas" and A.11.2, "Equipment". The next sections discuss each control one by one.

A.11.1 Secure Areas

Objective: To prevent unauthorized physical access, damage, and interference to the organization's information and information processing facilities.

Explanation: Prevent unauthorized physical access and prevent damage to the organizational site and information. This includes the office building, rooms, and the facilities such as air-conditioning, heating, electricity, etc.

This control is further broken down into six subparts.

A.11.1.1 Physical Security Perimeter

Control: Security perimeters should be defined and used to protect areas that contain either sensitive or critical information and information processing facilities.

Explanation: The boundaries of the organization must be secured and defined. The expectation here is to have a secure fence or building wall that can protect critical information from compromise. The sensitive assets can be kept under secured room and in lockers.

A.11.1.2 Physical Entry Controls

Control: Secure areas should be protected by appropriate entry controls to ensure that only authorized personnel are allowed access.

Explanation: The organizational secure areas such as entry gates, server rooms, and other important facilities are accessible by the authorized personnel only. All the sensitive entry areas should be identified. Here are some the tips to ensure no unauthorized access is allowed.

- Entry by personnel access control only. For example, by using biometric devices.

- Visitor entry must be recorded in a visitor logbook and they get temporary access to entry with a visitor card.

A.11.1.3 Securing Offices, Rooms, and Facilities

Control: Physical security of offices, rooms, and facilities should be designed and applied.

  Explanation: The security of offices, rooms, and other facilities is not usually a big challenge. They can be secured by implementing the basic security components. To implement this control, ask yourself some basic questions like these:

- Is access protected and revoked when not required?

- Is there a policy to remove the organizational asset after use if the rooms and facilities are shared among different organizations?

Note   The external auditor may inspect the offices, rooms, and facilities to check if there is evidence of risk-based control implementations.

A.11.1.4 Protecting Against External and Environmental Threats

Control: Physical protection against natural disasters, malicious attacks, or accidents should be designed and applied.

  Explanation: This control covers how you protect your organization from natural disasters and malicious attack or accidents. Here you need to identify potential natural or man-made disasters. Take a few examples of environmental threats such as floods, tornado, earthquake, lightning, fire, etc. Man-made threats can be water leakage from the company facility or any other things that make the environment difficult to work for the employees.

  The external auditor will check for evidence that you identified all the potential threats and vulnerabilities and you also accessed or treated the environmental risks.

Evidence that can be prepared:

- Proof showing the threats and vulnerability assessment are done properly.

- Mock fire drills videos can be presented as proof.

A.11.1.5 Working in Secure Areas

Control: Procedures for working in secure areas should be designed and applied.

Explanation: This control covers the procedures that can be established to secure the organization work areas. The external auditor can check for the procedure and/or policy document for secure areas, which should cover:

- Employees in and out time logging.

- Restriction of video/audio recording to sensitive areas within the organization.

- Restriction on unauthorized entry in office premises.

Evidence that can be prepared: A procedure or policy document for keeping work area secured. Also, the auditor can ask for supporting evidence.

A.11.1.6 Delivery and Loading Areas

Control: Access points such as delivery and loading areas and other points where unauthorized persons could enter the premises should be controlled and, if possible, isolated from information processing facilities to avoid unauthorized access.

Explanation: This control covers the delivery and loading areas protection. The focus is on keeping unauthorized people away from the processing information facilities and to keeping them in an isolated area if possible under the supervision of CCTV recording 24/7. If this control does not apply to your organization, it can be updated in the SOA (Statement of Applicability) document as Not Applicable.

Evidence that can be prepared: A procedure or policy document can be written which clearly defines who all can enter the delivery and loading premises.

A.11.2 Equipment

Objective: To prevent loss, damage, theft, or compromise of assets and interruption to the organization's operations.

   Explanation: So far, the various components of physical and environmental security have been covered. This section focuses on equipment. The goal of A.11.2 is to prevent loss, damage, theft, or compromise of assets and to protect from interruption of business operations. This control is further broken into nine subparts. The next sections discuss them one by one.

A.11.2.1 Equipment Siting and Protection

Control: Equipment should be sited and protected to reduce the risks from environmental threats and hazards, and opportunities for unauthorized access.

   Explanation: This control covers the protection of equipment from environmental threats and hazards and prevents unauthorized access. To reduce potential threats, risk assessment could be conducted. Here are some tips to safeguard equipment from unauthorized access:

- Storage facilities must be secured from unauthorized access. This can be attained by restricting keys only to authorized personnel.

- Laptops and desktops with sensitive data must be protected from the direct viewing angle.

- You must have a separate cafeteria for food and drink to keep them away from information processing facilities.

   Evidence that can be prepared: Clear desk/screen policy and the risk assessment document

   Who prepares it: The IT team is responsible for securing equipment siting and protection.

   For external audit: The external auditor conducting the ISO 27001 audit may ask for evidence.

A.11.2.2 Supporting Utilities (Control ISO 27001)

Equipment should be protected from power failures and other disruptions caused by failures in supporting utilities.

Explanation/what is required: You need to protect the supporting utilities from power failure. Supporting utilities include but not limited to electricity, telecommunications, water supply, gas, sewage, ventilation, and air conditioning. The following points to consider are:

- Test and inspect the supporting equipment regularly.

- Make sure that it conforms to manufacturer's specifications and local laws.

- If required, keep a backup ready for all types of equipment.

Evidence that can be prepared:

- Services and maintenance record.

- List of backup equipment if available

Who prepares it: The IT and the Admin teams are responsible for securing the supporting utilities and upkeep of records.

For external audit: The external auditor conducting the ISO 27001 audit may ask for this evidence.

A.11.2.3 Cabling Security (Control ISO 27001)

Power and telecommunications cabling carrying data or supporting information services should be protected from interception, interference, or damage.

Explanation/what is required: This control covers cabling security, which includes telecommunication wires and other cables to support the flow of information service. The following points should be considered:

- All the cables or wires should be underground where possible to protect them from damage.

- The electromagnetic shield can be used to protect the cables.

- Access to the patch panel and cable rooms should be protected and controlled.

Evidence that can be prepared: Access control to the cable/network room and maintenance and inspection record of cables.

Who prepares it: The IT team is responsible for the cabling security along with other relevant stakeholders if available.

For external audit: The external auditor may physically verify the cabling security and can ask for some evidence for maintenance and upkeep of cables.

A.11.2.4 Equipment Maintenance (Control ISO 27001)

Equipment should be correctly maintained to ensure its continued availability and integrity.

Explanation/what is required: This control covers the maintenance of equipment to ensure its availability and integrity. The following points can be considered:

- Only authorized maintenance personnel should be allowed to carry out repairs and service equipment.

- The equipment should be maintained following the supplier's recommended service intervals and specifications. For example, if the Genset manufacturer service term is every six months, and it should be done on time and records should be maintained.

Evidence to be prepared: Maintenance record for all equipment, list of assets under maintenance.

Who prepares it: The IT or Admin team is responsible for the regular maintenance of equipment.

For external audit: The external auditor conducting the ISO 27001 audit may ask for this evidence.

A.11.2.5 Removal of Assets (Control ISO 27001)

Equipment, information, or software should not be taken off-site without prior authorization.

Explanation/what is required: This is the security of equipment and any information or other equipment should not be taken off-site without authorization or approval from the relevant departments. Some key points for consideration are:

- When equipment is transferred to individuals or vendors off-premises, a log document should be maintained.

- Organizational equipment and media devices should not be left unattended in public.

Evidence that can be prepared: Gate pass for equipment taken off-premises.

Who prepares it: The IT team, along with the admin team, is responsible for securing the removal of assets.

For external audit: The external auditor conducting the ISO 27001 audit may ask for this evidence.

A.11.2.7 Secure Disposal or Reuse of Equipment (Control ISO 27001)

All items of equipment containing storage media should be verified to ensure that any sensitive data and licensed software has been removed or securely overwritten prior to disposal or re-use.

Explanation/what is required: This control covers the secure disposal of equipment. The important point is before reuse of any media device or equipment, all the sensitive data must be removed. Here are some points to consider:

- The encryption process should be strong and must cover the entire disk.

- The encryption key should be long enough to protect from any attack and be updated in the encryption policy.

- Never store the encryption key on the same disk. The key must be protected from unauthorized disclosure.

Evidence that can be prepared: Media disposal and reuse policy, and encryption policy

Who prepares it: The IT team is responsible for defining and documenting the media disposal and encryption policy along with other stakeholders.

For external audit: The external auditor conducting the ISO 27001 audit may ask for this evidence.

Note   Complete disk encryption reduces the risk of disclosure of confidential information when equipment is disposed of or reused.

A.11.2.8 Unattended User Equipment (Control ISO 27001)

Users should ensure that unattended equipment has appropriate protection.

Explanation/what is required: The control says that none of the equipment should be unattended in the organization and they must be protected. Here are some points to consider:

- Keep unattended equipment in the locker to protect them from unauthorized use.

- When the user is not at her desk, use automatic locking with password protection.

- Sessions must get terminated automatically if the user is not active in a predefined time frame.

Evidence that can be prepared: A log document for keys and drawers assigned to individuals and a session report from the server.

Who prepares it: The IT team is responsible for defining policy and procedure to protect unattended users' system or equipment.

For external audit: The external auditor may check for the list of keys or lockers allocated to individuals or may ask for related evidence.

A.11.2.9 Clear Desk and Clear Screen Policy (Control ISO 27001)

A clear desk policy for papers and removable storage media and a clear screen policy for information processing facilities should be adopted.

Explanation/what is required: This control covers the clear desk policy and must take care of physical papers, removable media, and the clear screen. The following points should be considered:

- Any business-critical information, either in the form of physical paper or storage media, must be kept in the locker.

- Unauthorized users should not have access to use photocopiers and scanners.

- A clear desk/clear screen policy helps in reducing the risks of unauthorized access and damage to information during and outside the office working hours.

Evidence that can be prepared: Clear desk and screen policy and an access control policy

Who prepares it: The IT team is responsible for defining the clear desk/screen policy.

For external audit: The external auditor conducting the ISO 27001 audit may ask for the evidence.

A.12 Operations Security

A.12.1 Operational Procedures and Responsibilities

Objective: To ensure correct and secure operations of information processing facilities.

Explanation/what is required: You need procedures to run operations smoothly and securely. The importance of defining and sharing standard operating procedures to all employees/contractors is communicated. Procedures should be defined by matching the business needs and objectives.

A.12.1.1 Documented Operating Procedures (ISO 27001 Control)

Operating procedures should be documented and made available to all users who need them.

Explanation/what is required: All the standard operating procedures related to business processes must be defined and made available to all the employees and contractors to perform the daily tasks in smooth and secure manner. This procedure will ensure that everybody understands their roles. It will help reduce the probability of information security risks happening.

Evidence that can be prepared: All the required standard operating procedures.

Who prepares it: All the department stakeholders will define the procedures with the help of the information security team.

For external audit: The external auditor conducting the ISO 27001 certification audit will check for the standard operating procedures, and determine how easily they are accessible for the employees who need them to execute the tasks as new employees keeps joining the company. They must be made aware of the path/portal from where they can access this information.

A.12.1.2 Change Management (ISO 27001 Control)

Change to the organization business processes, information processing facilities, and systems that affect information security should be controlled.

Explanation/what is required: Whenever a change occurs in the organization in terms of business processes or tools/applications, responsibilities etc., that change must be planned and executed in a controlled manner. When changes occur, it becomes important to re-analyze the security controls, as they might need changes too. All the security risks must be analyzed thoroughly for their potential impact on the security controls and appropriate approvals to be taken from the change control board (CCB) before implementing change management. Any security risk you skip can lead to a threat to the company information once it is released/implemented into the system.

Evidence that can be prepared:

- Change management procedures

- Change and impact analysis form

- Change log/tracker

Who prepares it: The information security department, with the help of the subject matter experts selected for the implementation team, should define the change management procedure, as it needs to cover all aspects of business operations. Concerned department stakeholders should prepare the change and impact analysis form and maintain the change log/tracker on a regular basis.

For external audit: The external auditor conducting the ISO 27001 certification audit will check for the change management procedures. They will confirm that the change control board is created to review/approve the changes before they are implemented and released into the system or business operations for employees/contractors to follow.

Also, the change and impact analysis form and the change log/tracker will be verified for any current changes.

A.12.1.3 Capacity Management (ISO 27001 Control)

The use of resources should be monitored and tuned, and projections made of future capacity requirements to ensure the required system performance.

Explanation/what is required: The requirement is whenever the IT systems reach their maximum capacity levels (such as server disk space). Overloaded systems usually don't run at optimum efficiency levels, which downgrades the service levels for your system users/customers, and it will directly impact the business. It is important to keep analyzing and monitoring the performance of your systems on a regular basis. Once you start analyzing the usage of your systems, you need to forecast whether there is any need to upgrade the systems in terms of numbers or capacity to deliver the optimum performance levels.

Evidence that can be prepared:

- Capacity management procedures. Tools/applications implemented that must detect and communicate systems usage for server disk space.

  This will help to perform the following tasks:

  - If disk space is full, then you have to delete obsolete data to create space.

  - You may have to decommission some of the systems/applications that are no longer in use or needed to provide any services.

  - You need to identify services that are not critical and restricting their bandwidth, such as for video streaming.

- Capacity management projections plan document.

Who prepares it: The information security department, with the help of the subject matter expects selected for the implementation team, should define the capacity management procedure, as it needs to cover all aspects of the business.

For external audit: The external auditor conducting the ISO 27001 certification audit will check for the capacity management procedures, to check how capacity management I monitored, forecasted, and planned for the systems to deliver optimum performance levels.

A.12.1.4 Separation of Development, Testing, and Operational Environment (ISO 27001 Control)

Development, testing, and operational environments should be separated to reduce the risks of anybody having unauthorized access or changes to the operational environment.

Explanation/what is required: The requirement is to maintain the development, testing, and operational environments separately, employees/contractors working on these environments their access must be checked and controlled, so that they do not perform any unauthorized actions or changes in the system. These must be detectable easily for all the verification and future audit purposes, as any incident occurs this information is always helpful.

Evidence that can be prepared: The environment creation procedures. The following are some points that can be used to create the guidelines:

- Define the rules for how software would be transferred from one environment to another, for example, from the development to operation/production environment.

- Define the access levels for each environment and how to monitor them. For example, developer access to operation/production environment must be prohibited, as it can pose a threat of unauthorized changes or modification to the software code or operations/production data.

- Different environments must be run on different systems or computers.

- Changes to the operating systems or the applications must be tested in a testing or staging environment before implemented in the operation environment. Testing must be avoided on the operation/ production environment.

- Organizations based on their business needs should analyze and cover their required security controls for the creation of stable and secure environments.

- Project management plan defines employees who will have access permissions to work on the different environments.

- Separate environments should be created and maintained for development, testing, and operations.

Who prepares it: The information security department, with the help of the subject matter expects selected for the implementation team, should define the environment creation guideline.

Project managers should define all the access controls for all the different environments for their project team members. Access control reviews must be performed on a regular basis and records must be maintained.

The IT helpdesk team creates and maintains separate environments for development, testing, and operations.

For external audit: The external auditor conducting the ISO 27001 certification audit will check for the environment creation guideline, to check how the environment is created and access control levels are planned, given, and monitored on a regular basis.

A.12.2 Protection from Malware

Objective: To ensure that information and information processing facilities are rotected against malware.

Explanation/what is required: The organization and employees must know how to detect and protect their organization information from malware attacks. Employees must know what malware is and how it can be harmful.

A.12.2.1 Controls Against Malware (ISO 27001 Control)

Detection, prevention, and recovery controls to protect against malware should be implemented, combined with appropriate user awareness.

Explanation/what is required: As you are aware, malware is a serious threat so organizations must analyze and implement appropriate security controls, including educating the employees on a regular basis to prevent malware attacks. It is important that organizations install malware detection software as it will scan all the incoming data and will block any malware threat. The malware detection software may not be able to protect your systems in all the scenarios, so the focus must be more on prevention methods.

Consider the following points when implementing the controls:

- The organization should define a policy to communicate to the employees/contractors that the use of any unauthorized software/ tools is prohibited.

- Use controls that help in the prevention and detection of unauthorized software.

- Use controls that help in the prevention and detection of websites that are malicious or could spread malicious content, i.e. sites that are blacklisted.

- Install malware detection software to prevent and block malware threats. As a preventive measure, schedule the scan of all computer systems and media to detect malware. Scan files received over the network or through storage media, email attachments, and web pages. Regular updates to the software should be done to address the latest malware threats.

- Plan and perform the regular reviews of your organization's systems to check whether any unauthorized or prohibited files/software exist, which could pose a malware threat.

- Plan regular training/awareness sessions for the employees/ contractors so that they can prevent malware attacks.

Evidence that can be prepared: An authorized software usage policy to prohibit employees from using any unauthorized/unapproved software/tools. An antivirus policy because all systems must be installed with the antivirus/antimalware software to prevent any form of information security attack.

Standard operating procedures could be prepared that can guide teams during a malware attack as what should be done and what the responsibilities are of employees/ resolution teams. Also, it could be the part of business continuity planning as well, as if systems are down due to a malware attack then how to recover from it, for e.g. all crucial/ important data and software is backed up and could be restored faster to make your organizations systems up and running.

Records of scan results showing prevention/detection/removal of malware.

Employee training/awareness plan and participation evidence i.e. training attendees and training material etc.

Records of regular patch updates to the malware/antivirus detection software.

Who prepares it: The information security department, with the help of the IT Helpdesk team, which is part of implementation team, should define the policies and procedures.

The IT Helpdesk team maintains all the records of scan results, showing prevention/ detection/removal of malware. It also patches the update records. The information security team maintains the employees training/awareness plan and the training participation records.

For external audit: The external auditor conducting the ISO 27001 certification audit will check for the policies and procedures. Malware/antivirus software installed on organization systems/machines should be up to date and working. Records of scan results/regular patch updates. Employee training evidence.

A.12.3 Backup

Objective: To protect against the loss of data.

Explanation/what is required: The requirement is to identify and implement controls to prevent the loss of company information.

A.12.3.1 Information Backup (ISO 27001 Control)

Backup copies of information, software, and system images should be taken and tested regularly in accordance with an agreed backup policy.

Explanation/what is required: Organizations must define a backup policy that can be followed to prevent the loss of data. The policy should cover how the backup activities will be done to protect the information. Once the data backup is done, it needs to be stored. It is important to define how the data will be stored on tapes, on cloud, etc. Also, how long will the data be retained, such as for or years or seven years, for example. The backup data must be tested on a regular basis to check whether it can be restored easily and is working as required.

As per the ISO 27001 standard it is the requirement that backup data/information be stored far from the main office site/location, to protect it from any type of damage due to natural unexpected disaster at the main office, this will help also help to restore the data safely whenever required. Also, the site or location where the data would be kept for storage must be access controlled, and no unauthorized individuals should be allowed to gain access. The location should be compliant to standard security requirements (fire proof, able to handle floods/earthquake, etc.).

Note   These days, organizations hire vendors to provide services to manage and safeguard their backup data in tapes or at datacenters.

The organization should analyze and define their own backup policy/procedure. As each organization can have different requirements, some may require real-time imaging of the data as they might be processing financial transaction.

Evidence that can be prepared:

- Backup policy

- Backup restoration procedure

- Backup plan

- Backup restoration test records

- Agreement with vendor, if you're hiring a vendor for maintaining data tapes and/or datacenters

- Audit of vendor to check all safety controls are implemented to safeguard organization data

Who prepares it: The information security department with the help of the IT Helpdesk team, which is part of implementation team, should define the policies and procedures.

The IT Helpdesk team should do the following:

- Maintain all the backup records to confirm data restoration was successful. Whenever restoration was unsuccessful, document what actions were taken. Have an agreement with the vendor for the storage of backup tapes and for datacenter services.

- Information security team conducts the audit along with the IT Helpdesk team at the vendor site, to ensure they are compliant and are meeting the organizational requirements.

For external audit: The external auditor conducting the ISO 27001 certification audit will check for the policies and procedures. They check how the back procedure is followed as a practice in the organization and whether it is compliant as per the ISO 27001 standards.

A.12.4 Logging and Monitoring

Objective: To record events and generate evidence.

Explanation/what is required: Identify and implement controls to record the events of employee/contractor systems who were attempting to gain unauthorized access to files or systems. This is a security threat and may result in the loss of company information.

A.12.4.1 Event Logging (ISO 27001 Control)

Event logs recording user activities, exceptions, faults, and information security events should be produced, kept, and regularly reviewed.

Explanation/what is required: Organizations must create the provisions and implement security controls so that they can record all the user activities that they are doing on the organization systems allotted to them. This ensures that they are not misusing or trying to gain any unauthorized access or sharing the information outside the organization. This will be stored in the form of event logs.

Apart from the user/employee activities, it is also important to know if there are any system level faults/errors or exceptions scenarios. This information could also be available via the stored event logs.

Note   What all should event logs must store or display is in the ISO 27002:2013 code of practice. The list is very long, so it is not covered here.

Evidence that can be prepared:

- Event management procedure
- Event logs
- Event logs analysis record (with actions taken)
- List of systems/devices configured for monitoring

Who prepares it: The IT Helpdesk team can prepare all the evidence/documents by consulting the information security team.

For external audit: The external auditor conducting the ISO 27001 certification audit will check the procedure and records in order to understand how user activities and system faults/errors are tracked and monitored.

A.12.4.2 Protection of Log Information (ISO 27001 Control)

Logging facilities and log information should be protected against tampering and unauthorized access.

Explanation/what is required: Organizations must create the provisions and implement security controls to prevent the logs from being tampered with. If these logs are tampered with, the purpose of storing them would not make sense.

Hence, it is important to detect whenever there are changes or deletions to the logs. Also, you may need to monitor if there is enough storage space to record all the log events. If there is a space issue then log information may be overwritten.

Evidence that can be prepared: Implemented security tools that will help to detect and record the logs of unauthorized changes or access to the logs monitor the disk space left to record the logs without any interruption.

Who prepares it: The IT Helpdesk team can prepare all the evidence/records by consulting with the information security team.

For external audit: The external auditor conducting the ISO 27001 certification audit will check the controls/records in order to understand how logs are protected from being tampered and from unauthorized access.

A.12.4.3 Administrator and Operator Logs (ISO 27001 Control)

System administrator and system operator activities should be logged, and the logs should be protected and regularly reviewed.

Explanation/what is required: Organizations must create the provisions and implement security controls to prevent logs from being tampered with by the employees who are designated as the administrator. They could modify the log data which is an information security breach.

Evidence that can be prepared: Implemented security tools help to detect and record the logs of administrator activities and a regular review of administrator activities logs.

Who prepares it: The IT Helpdesk team can prepare all the evidence/records by consulting the information security team.

For external audit: The external auditor conducting the ISO 27001 certification audit will check the controls/records in order to understand how administrator logs are protected.

A.12.4.4 Clock synchronization (ISO 27001 Control)

The clocks of all relevant information processing systems within an organization or security domain should be synchronized to a single reference time source.

Explanation/what is required: Organizations must ensure that the clocks of all the information processing systems within their organization/scope are automatically synchronized with an accurate time source. It is very important that time source is reliable because the purpose is to record the accurate timestamps of the security events that occur in your organization on a specific day/time.

Hence, these logs and records are required for investigation purposes internally due to disciplinary issues or could be required by the legal authorities. Because of this it is important that all computer clocks and telephone systems must display accurate time, and this can be done through network time protocol mechanism, which will help to synchronize clocks on computers, across networks (Internet or local area networks—LANs and all the servers).

Evidence that can be prepared:

- Clock synchronization procedure

- Test/review records of the computer systems, audit/incident logs displaying correct time based on the correct time source

Who prepares it: The IT Helpdesk team can prepare all the evidence/records by consulting the information security team.

For external audit: The external auditor conducting the ISO 27001 certification audit will check the controls/records in order to verify whether all information processing systems of the organization are displaying the correct clock synchronization from a reliable time source.

A.12.5 Control of Operational Software

Objective: To ensure the integrity of operational systems.

Explanation/what is required: Identify and implement controls to prevent the installation of unauthorized software on computers or any other operating systems.

A.12.5.1 Installation of Software on Operational Systems (ISO 27001 Control)

Procedures should be implemented to control the installation of software on operational systems.

Explanation/what is required: Organizations must create provisions and implement security controls so that they can prevent employees/contractors from installing software that is unauthorized/unapproved. It must be done only by the trained administrator once they receive approval from authorizing body members.

The main purpose of preventing such installations is to avoid any security threat/attack. If employee/contractor installs any malicious software on their allotted computer systems, it could pose a big threat and would become easier for any hacker to install malware.

Hence, it is advisable that computer systems of employee/contractors not bee allowed to install software. Employees must be routed to a Helpdesk system to log a request to install required software. The request then must be approved by the requestor immediate supervisor and to a final approver who has authority to accept or reject the request upon assessing the security threat that might occur.

It is very important that organizations/teams assess all the scenarios i.e. operational and security related before implementing any software changes to the operational systems. Whenever any new software version changes and must be installed, teams must have the rollback plan and must retain previous versions of the software as a contingency. Hence it is advisable that all new software and new versions of software be thoroughly tested on individual systems first to assess any problems before declaring them as fit for implementation and use.

Evidence that can be prepared:

- Software installation policy

- Software installation procedure

- Security controls implemented to prohibit users from installing software on their own

- Regular review/audit records of systems, to verify that unauthorized/ unapproved software is not installed on computer systems/or any other devices

Who prepares it: The IT Helpdesk team can prepare all the evidence/records by consulting the information security team.

For external audit: The external auditor conducting the ISO 27001 certification audit will check the policy/procedure/security controls/records in order to verify that unauthorized/unapproved software is not installed on computer systems/or any other devices by the employees/contractors and only trained administrator have installed them upon acquiring the necessary approvals.

A.12.6 Technical Vulnerability Management

Objective: To prevent exploitation of technical vulnerabilities.

Explanation/what is required: Identify and implement controls to detect the technical vulnerabilities in the organization information processing systems and prevent these identified vulnerabilities form being exploited by an external source i.e. a hacker or an insider within your organization. Let's look at this further in the control explained next.

A.12.6.1 Management of Technical Vulnerabilities (ISO 27001 Control)

Information about technical vulnerabilities of information systems being used should be obtained in a timely fashion. The organization's exposure to such vulnerabilities should be evaluated and appropriate measures taken to address the associated risk.

Explanation/what is required: Organizations must create the provisions and implement security controls so that they can prevent the exploitation of the identified technical vulnerabilities. Before proceeding further, it is important to understand what vulnerability is.

Organizations must do the following for the management of technical vulnerabilities:

- Roles and responsibilities should be defined for managing the vulnerabilities i.e. their regular monitoring, assessment of risks due to identified threats, patch management, and asset tracking. It is important to prepare the list of assets, which organization is using. The purpose is to know where they are installed and who their owner is, what are their current versions and configuration, etc.

- Organizations must procure and deploy tools that can help to identify vulnerabilities, such as tools to detect network vulnerabilities and vulnerabilities in software applications. Once identified, they must be analyzed for potential threats, and the ones which are high must be addressed first and in a timely manner.

- Organizations must perform vulnerability tests on a regular basis, as new vulnerabilities keep arising and teams must be ready to take the necessary actions, whenever required.

Each vulnerability will be different depending on the business or domain they are responsible for. Technical teams/experts must analyze and perform tests accordingly.

Evidence that can be prepared:

- Vulnerability assessment policy

- Vulnerability management procedure

- Vulnerability test records/action plans

- Risk register with risks identified during vulnerability testing

Who prepares it: The IT Helpdesk team for network vulnerability testing and for application vulnerability could be a separate technical team of experts. They can prepare all the evidence/records by consulting the information security team.

For external audit: The external auditor conducting the ISO 27001 certification audit will check the policy/procedure/security controls/records. They verify that organizations are detecting vulnerabilities and are taking necessary actions on a regular basis to secure organization information processing systems.

A.12.6.2 Restrictions on Software Installation (ISO 27001 Control)

Rules governing the installation of software by users should be established and implemented.

Explanation/what is required: Organizations must create the provisions and implement security controls to restrict the users/employees to install software on their computer systems. Organizations can create the list of software that the user/employee can install. The list must be communicated to reduce the risk of any threats arising from unapproved/unauthorized software installation.

For this control to work effectively, users/employees must be provided with least privileges. These privileges should be provided based on the user/employee role and must be monitored on a regular basis.

Evidence that can be prepared:

- Software installation policy

- List of software allowed to be installed by the users/employees

- List of users with privileges

- Vulnerability test records/action plans

- Risk register with risks identified during vulnerability testing

Who prepares it: The IT Helpdesk team can prepare all the evidence/records by consulting the information security team.

For external audit: The external auditor conducting the ISO 27001 certification audit will check the policy/procedure/security controls/records. They verify how organizations have implemented the controls to restrict the users/employees from installing any software.

A.12.7 Information Systems Audit Considerations

Objective: To minimize the impact of audit activities on operational systems.

Explanation/what is required: Identify and reduce the impact on organization systems due to the audit requirements.

A.12.7.1 Information system audit controls (ISO 27001 Control)

Audit requirements and activities involving verification of operational systems should be carefully planned and agreed to minimize disruptions to business processes.

Explanation/what is required: Though audit is a mandatory exercise for any organization, it should be planned carefully to minimize the disruptions to the operations and its systems, which might occur during the audit verification exercise.

Consider the following points to minimize the impact:

- The plan on the access requirements should be provided on the information and the systems to the auditors.

- Audit scope must be agreed and communicated to the auditees, so that auditees showcase information/evidence only for the agreed scope.

- Wherever possible, give read only access to software and data to perform the audit tests.

- Some audit tests that require longer hours must be planned after business/operation hours/shifts.

- Access permissions provided for the audit must be monitored and logs should be maintained for future verification purposes.

Evidence that can be prepared:

- Audit policy

- Audit scope/audit plan

- Audit reports

- List of users provided access for audit purposes

- Recorded users log of system access for audit/test purposes

Who prepares it: The IT Helpdesk team can prepare all the evidence/records by consulting the information security team.

For external audit: The external auditor conducting the ISO 27001 certification audit will check the policy/procedure/security controls/records. To verify how organizations has implemented the controls to minimize the impact on operations/ systems due to audit verification exercises.

A.13 Communication Security

A.13.1 Network Security Management

Objective: To ensure the protection of information in networks and the supporting information processing facilities.

Explanation/what is required: Control and determine which users can access network data.

A.13.1.1 Network Controls (ISO 27001 Control)

Networks should be managed and controlled to protect information in systems and applications.

Explanation/what is required: The organization can do the following to implement network control measures:

- Establish the procedures and clear responsibilities for managing the network equipment.

- Implement controls to safeguard the information that travels over the network to protect the systems and applications running on the network.

- Maintain network activity logs and monitor them on a regular basis.

181

Evidence that can be prepared:

- Access control policy

- Network control policy

- Procedure for managing network equipment

- Risk tracker (with identified risks as part of access permissions)

Who prepares it: The information security team needs to get input from various departments, including critical ones like the IT Helpdesk team, to define the access control policy.

For external audit: The external auditor conducting the ISO 27001 certification audit will check the evidence in order to verify how the organization has defined and communicated the policy to all stakeholders.

A.13.1.2 Security of Network Services (ISO 27001 Control)

Security mechanisms, service levels, and management requirements of all network services should be identified and included in network services agreements, whether these services are provided in-house or outsourced.

Explanation/what is required: Organizations hire network service providers for their Internet service requirements, it is important to assess whether service providers are capable to provide Internet services by following secure methods. To minimize information security risks and its impact, organizations must have network services agreement signed with the service provider by clearly defining the required service levels.

Evidence that can be prepared:

- Access control policy

- Network control policy

- Network services agreement

- Risk tracker (with identified risks, assessed as part of network service agreement)

Who prepares it:

- The information security team facilitates in defining the network control policy by getting input from the IT Helpdesk team.

- The IT Helpdesk team defines the network services agreement

- Legal team reviews/approves the network services agreement after analyzing the information security risks

For external audit: The external auditor conducting the ISO 27001 certification audit will check the network services agreement done with the network service provider. They verify how the organization has defined the agreement with the vendor to safeguard their organization information.

A.13.1.3 Segregation in Networks (ISO 27001 Control)

Groups of information services, users, and information systems should be segregated on networks.

Explanation/what is required: Segregate them to make them work separately in a secure manner, because this way it will not be easy for hackers to identify the structure of your organization network and will help in preventing network intrusion attacks. The main aim of network segregation is to put restrictions on accessing sensitive information, hosts, and services. Hence, segregation measures must be assessed as per the access control policy before implementation, as it can impact the network performance.

The organization can do the following to segregate the networks:

- Create separate network domains by assessing each domain trust level.

- For each domain, define its perimeter as it helps to control the access between network domains using a gateway.

- Organizations must put more focus on wireless networks as they are to be considered as external connections. Access to the sensitive/confidential information over wireless network is not to be allowed unless and until it is allowed by the firewall as per meeting the defined set rules and network control policy.

Evidence that can be prepared:

- Network control policy

- Access control policy

- Network diagram showing segregated network

Who prepares it: The information security team facilitates in defining the network control policy by getting input from the IT Helpdesk team. The IT Helpdesk team defines the network diagram showing the segregated network.

For external audit: The external auditor conducting the ISO 27001 certification audit will check the evidence to verify how the organization has done the networks segregation to restrict the access for preventing network intrusion attacks.

A.13.2 Information Transfer

Objective: To maintain the security of information transferred within an organization and with any external entity.

Explanation: Put controls for transfer of information within and outside the information.

A.13.2.1 Information Transfer Policies and Procedures (ISO 27001 Control)

Formal transfer policies, procedures, and controls should be in place to protect the transfer of information using all types of communication facilities.

Explanation/what is required: Organizations should define policies and procedures for implementing controls in safeguarding the transfer of information by employees/contractors at work.

The points to consider for implementing controls are:

- Be able to detect malware that could be transmitted while using electronic mode of communication.

- Be able to protect sensitive information that is shared as an attachment.

- Frame policy or guideline that explains how to use communication facilities in a secure manner at work.

- Apply cryptographic techniques.

- Conduct awareness sessions for employees on a regular basis and tell them to remain cautious while speaking at public places to prevent sharing of any confidential information.

Organizations can identify many more controls, by assessing the tools/equipment used for transferring the information. As tools/technologies keep changing, you need to always assess risks to prevent mistakes and breaches while using them, as any security incident may also lead to legal implications.

Evidence that can be prepared:

- Information transfer policy

- Information transfer procedure

- Implemented controls

Who prepares it: The information security team helps define the information transfer policy and procedure by getting input from the IT Helpdesk team. The IT Helpdesk team implements the security controls.

For external audit: The external auditor conducting the ISO 27001 certification audit will check the evidence. They verify how security controls are implemented for safeguarding transfer of information via various modes of communication.

A.13.2.2 Agreements on Information Transfer (ISO 27001 Control)

Agreements should address the secure transfer of business information between the organization and external parties.

Explanation/what is required: Organizations communicate not only within their employees/offices, but also outside their organization with external parties. Hence to make sharing the information secure, it is important to frame agreements that cover secure transfer of information between your organization and external party. That way, they become responsible and liable to protect your organization information from any information security breach. Points to consider for framing the agreements are:

- The responsibilities of management in controlling and transfer of information

- The act of tracing the information from the source to destination

- Standards to follow for information packaging. For example, if courier services are required, what security standards will the courier firm follow to secure your information.

- If there is a security incident, how will issues be addressed, including any liabilities to be paid.

- Ensuring information classification is understood. The information access control levels must be agreed on by your organization and the external party.

Evidence that can be prepared:

- Information transfer policy

- Information transfer agreements

Who prepares it: The information security team facilitates in defining the information transfer policy and agreements. Before agreements are finalized they must be reviewed and approved by the legal team to prevent any liabilities of the organization during an information security breach.

For external audit: The external auditor conducting the ISO 27001 certification audit will check the evidence in order to verify how agreements are framed and what controls are covered as part of the agreement.

A.13.2.3 Electronic Messaging (ISO 27001 Control)

Information involved in electronic messaging should be appropriately protected.

Explanation/what is required: Organizations must create provisions to safeguard the information that's shared via electronic messaging. Consider the following points:

- No unauthorized access to the information/electronic messages. For example, if public services—i.e., instant messaging, social networking or file sharing—need to be used to share information, approvals must be received before using them.

There could be many more areas, which an organization must assess before allowing the use of electronic messaging.

Evidence that can be prepared: Electronic messaging policy

Who prepares it: The information security team will facilitate in defining the electronic messaging policy in discussion with the IT/Helpdesk team.

For external audit: The external auditor conducting the ISO 27001 certification audit will check the evidence in order to verify how the electronic messaging policy is defined and implemented in your organization.

A.13.2.4 Confidentiality or Non-Disclosure Agreements (ISO 27001 Control)

Requirements for confidentiality or non-disclosure agreements reflecting the organization needs for the protection of information should be identified, regularly reviewed, and documented.

Explanation/what is required: Organizations must create non-disclosure agreements (NDAs), either with external parties or with the employees as required, to protect the company information. NDAs cover the legal aspects to make the parties liable for protecting the information.

Points to consider in the non-disclosure agreement are:

- Information to be protected

- Responsibilities of the parties/organizations in safeguarding the information

- Duration of the agreement; how long the information must be protected

- Right to audit any external parties (vendors/suppliers, etc.)

There could be many more points, which an organization must assess before finalizing on the non-disclosure agreement

Evidence that can be prepared: Non-disclosure agreement

Who prepares it: The legal team will facilitate in defining/reviewing and finalizing the non-disclosure agreement.

For external audit: The external auditor conducting the ISO 27001 certification audit will check the evidence in order to verify how the non-disclosure agreement is defined and shared/signed with external parties or with employees to safeguard company information.

A.14 System Acquisition, Development, and Maintenance

A.14.1 Security Requirements of Information Systems

Objective: To ensure that information security is an integral part of information systems across the entire lifecycle. This includes the requirements for information systems that provide services over public networks.

Explanation: This control covers the lifecycle of the information system and it is an important part of ISMS. The next sections discuss each control one by one.

A.14.1.1 Information Security Requirements Analysis and Specification (Control ISO 27001)

The information security-related requirements should be included in the requirements for new information systems or enhancements to existing information systems.

Explanation/what is required: You need to identify the security-related requirements. For example, if you have a new requirement to build an ecommerce portal, the security requirements must be identified such as SSL certificate and payment using secured TLS (Transport Layer Security). Some points of the information security requirement that you should consider are:

- Access provisioning and permission for business users, technical users, and other user groups.

- The requirements mandated by other security controls, for example, interfaces for logging and monitoring or data leakage detection systems.

- Security requirements to be collected in a separate section for each project/product.

- The criteria for product acceptance should be defined before the UAT (User Acceptance Testing) to assure the customer that security requirements are met.

Evidence that can be prepared: Requirements document with security requirements and test records

Who prepares it: The requirements document should be prepared by the software development team along with relevant stakeholders.

For external audit: The external auditor will look for the evidence of security requirements. For example, the requirement document can be checked for whether you are covering the security requirement or not.

A.14.1.2 Securing Application Services on Public Networks (Control ISO 27001)

The information involved in application services passing over public networks should be protected from fraudulent activity, contract dispute, and unauthorized disclosure and modification.

Explanation/what is required: The software application uses lots of data and these data travel on public networks. This control covers the security of application services over the public network. For example, the video learning platform wants to restrict the download of paid videos on a public network and this becomes one of the security requirements.

Some points to consider here:

- Authentication of registered users. Only authorized users can see the information.

- The payment page should verify the payment information from the supplied vendor.

Note   The controls required often include cryptographic methods for authentication and securing data transfer.

Evidence that can be prepared: Network security evidence such monitoring logs and authentication mechanism

Who prepares it: The software development team along with the IT team is responsible for preparing the required evidence along with relevant stakeholders.

For external audit: The auditor may check for security events logs, payment logs, and system error logs.

A.14.1.3 Protecting Application Services Transactions (Control ISO 27001)

The information involved in application service transactions should be protected to prevent incomplete transmission, misrouting, unauthorized message alteration, unauthorized disclosure, and unauthorized message duplication or replay.

Explanation/what is required: This control covers the application services transactions to secure the transactional information from any alteration and unauthorized disclosure. Some points to consider are:

- The transaction ensures that the user's secret authentication information is valid and remains confidential.

- The communication channel of all involved individuals is encrypted.

- Wherever required trusted authority is used. For example, the use of digital signatures and certificates.

Evidence that can be prepared: Payment logs, digital signatures and certificates

Who prepares it: The IT and software development teams are responsible for the security of application services.

For external audit: The external auditor may check for storage of certificates and ask for the logs and enquire about what kind of encryption tools are used.

A.14.2 Security in Development and Support Processes

Objective: To ensure that information security is designed and implemented within the development lifecycle of information systems.

Explanation: The objective is to ensure security in the design and within the development lifecycle of the information systems. There are multiple subcontrols for security in development.

A.14.2.1 Secure development policy (Control ISO 27001)

Rules for the development of software and systems should be established and applied to developments within the organization.

Explanation/what is required: This control covers the secure development policy. What controls should be established to make the development environment secure? The following points can be considered:

- Guidelines for secure coding practice for each programming language. For example, the name of any class should be written in camel case. Use of specific coding tools such as PhpStrom IDE, Eclipse, Netbeans, etc.

- Security requirements review at the end of each development phase.

- A secure repository and version control for code. For example, SVN, GitHub, etc.

Note   The developers should be trained for use and testing and code review. Reliable programming methods should be used for new developments and in code re-use scenarios.

Evidence that can be prepared: A secure code repository and version control. The coding guidelines for each programming language used in the organization.

Who prepares it: The software development team is responsible for preparing the coding guidelines and the IT/Infrastructure team is responsible for keeping the development environment secure.

For external audit: The external auditor will try to understand how you are securing your development environment and how the version control is done.

A.14.2.2 System Change Control Procedures (Control ISO 27001)

Changes to systems within the development lifecycle should be controlled using formal change control procedures.

Explanation/what is required: Change is inevitable in any software project and this control explains how to manage the changes within the development lifecycle. Some points for consideration:

- Keep records of approved changes by authorized users

- Maintain version control for all the approved changes

- Manage change within the software development lifecycle=

Evidence that can be prepared:

- Audit trail of all the changes. The software development team needs to prepare RTM (Requirement Traceability Matrix) and can document changes.

- Change log/tracker can be prepared.

Who prepares it: The software development is responsible for preparing the evidence document and other required controls.

For external audit: The external auditor can ask for a change-log document and/or the procedure to manage changes within the software development lifecycle.

A.14.2.3 Technical Review of Applications after Operating Platform Changes (Control ISO 27001)

When operating platforms are changed, business-critical applications should be reviewed and tested to ensure there is no adverse impact on organizational operations or security.

Explanation/what is required: The control covers how the technical review is performed once the operating system is changed. Sometimes changing the operating system may introduce security impacts or the code might not work as expected. The following points can be considered:

- Thorough testing needs to be done when the operating system gets changed.

- All the changes must be done to ensure that business continuity isn't impacted.

Note The operating platform includes databases, middleware, and any hardware or software version change. For example, an application developed in MySQL version 5.5 and deployed in version 5.7 must go through technical review and rigorous testing.

Evidence that can be prepared: Test case document and test results

Who prepares it: The software development team is responsible for the technical review of the application after a change in the operating platform.

For external audit: The external auditor may ask for a test case document or evidence of technical review.

Restrictions on Changes to Software Packages (Control ISO 27001)

Modifications to software packages should be discouraged, limited to necessary changes and all changes should be strictly controlled.

Explanation/what is required: The control covers the security controls of software packages. Unauthorized users should not be able to modify any software packages and it should have an access control placed by the IT team. Some points for consideration are:

- The software update should be done after verification of changes made in the patch.

- Only licensed software should be used and to be kept up to date.

- A software update policy can be prepared and procedure to update, frequency of update, validity testing, etc. should be defined.

Evidence that can be prepared:

- List of all licensed software

- Log to be maintained for patch updates

- Automatic system update logs

- Restriction implemented on systems for prohibiting users from installing software an their systems

Who prepares it: The IT team is responsible for managing software update restrictions and for maintaining the evidence.

For external audit: The external auditor may ask for the list of the licensed software and should be able to see how the policy is implemented to restrict the software update by unauthorized personnel.

A.14.2.5 Secure System Engineering Principles (Control ISO 27001)

Principles for engineering secure systems should be established, documented, maintained, and applied to any information system implementation efforts.

Explanation/what is required: The control explains the requirement of having a secure system engineering principle. For example, secure coding guideline to be followed by the development team to make the application development reliable and secure. The following points can be taken into consideration:

- All new technology should be analyzed for security risk and known attack pattern. For example, SQL injection is a known attack pattern in the database and hence those risk should be identified and worked on.

- If the development is outsourced to a third party vendor, then there must be some agreement or legal binding in place to force security measures.

- Perform code review to identify security related issues.

Note   The software development team should also follow the secure engineering principle such as user authentication, secure sessions, data validation, and other standard practices to keep their application and software product secure.

Evidence that can be prepared: Coding guidelines for all programming languages. Peer code review process can be defined and documented.

Who prepares it: The software development team is responsible for establishing secure engineering principles.

For external audit: The auditor may ask for the guidelines you use to protect the code from unauthorized access and may ask for some related evidence.

A.14.2.6 Secure Development Environment (Control ISO 27001)

Organizations should establish and appropriately protect secure development environments for system development and integration efforts that cover the entire system development lifecycle.

Explanation/what is required: The control covers the security of the development environment. This includes people, processes, and associated technology for development integration.

Organizations should assess risks associated with individual system development efforts and establish secure development environments for specific system development efforts. For example, to control the security of code, multiple environments can be set according to the requirement such as development environment, test environment, production environment. The following points need to be considered:

- The sensitivity of data and storage over different environments.

- Segregation of data between different development environments.

- Access control to the development environment. For example, the access to DBA can be all rights whereas developers only need view-only rights to the production database.

Evidence that can be prepared: Segregation of development environment. Secure code repository. Procedure for code deployment from one development environment to another.

Who prepares it: The software development team is responsible for maintaining the secure development environment.

For external audit: The auditor may check the evidence for segregation of development environment.

A.14.2.7 Outsourced Development (Control ISO 27001)

The organization should supervise and monitor the activity of outsourced system development

Example/what is required: This control covers the outsourced development security and the following points should be considered:

- Code ownership and intellectual copyright related to outsourced development.

- Acceptance testing for the quality and accuracy of software deliverables.

- Complete documentation deliverables.

- Company who outsourced the development have full rights to audit the development cycle.

Evidence that can be prepared:

- Agreement between both the parties

- The complete list of software deliverables

- Test results

- Audit results

Who prepares it: Management, along with relevant stakeholders, will be responsible for agreement along with the legal team and the software development team for test results and audit.

For external audit: The auditor may check the agreement or legal binding document between both parties.

A.14.2.8 System Security Testing (Control ISO 27001)

Testing the security functionality should be carried out during development.

Explanation/what is required: This control covers system security testing, which is performed during the development cycle. The security testing should be performed rigorously for the development project. Independent software testing should be performed for the acceptance of software application/product.

Evidence that can be prepared: Security test cases for the application/software product and security test results.

Who prepares it: The software development team is responsible for security testing of software development.

For external audit: The external auditor conducting the ISO 27001 audit can ask for the evidence.

A.14.2.9 System Acceptance Testing (Control ISO 27001)

Acceptance testing programs and related criteria should be established for new information systems, upgrades, and new versions.

Explanation/what is required: System acceptance testing should include testing of information security requirements. Organizations can leverage automated tools such as code scanner and vulnerability assessment.

Evidence that can be prepared: Security test cases and user acceptance test result

Who prepares it: The IT/Software development team is responsible for system acceptance testing.

For external audit: The external auditor conducting the ISO 27001 audit may check the security test case and results.

A.14.3 Test Data

Objective: To ensure the protection of data used for testing.

Explanation: This control ensures the protection of test data that is used for testing.

A.14.3.1 Protection of Test Data (Control ISO 27001)

Test data should be selected carefully, protected, and controlled.

Explanation/what is required: You need to protect the test data that can be your data. It is advisable not to use any of your personally identifiable data for test purposes. The following points should be implemented to protect operational data when used for testing purposes:

- The access control policy should also be implemented on the test application.

- The test data entered or copied should have an audit trail.

Evidence that can be prepared: Test data and audit trail log for test data

Who prepares it: The software development team is responsible for the protection of test data.

For external audit: The external auditor conducting the ISO 27001 audit may ask for audit tail log of test data or other related evidence.

A.15 Supplier Relationships

A.15.1 Information Security in Supplier Relationships

Objective: To ensure protection of an organization's assets that are accessible by suppliers.

Explanation/what is required: Organizations must assess information security risks. When they provide suppliers access to information and assets, there must be provisions to protect them from unauthorized access.

A.15.1.1 Information Security Policy for Supplier Relationships (ISO 27001 Control)

Information security requirements for mitigating the risks associated with supplier's access to the organization's assets should be agreed with the supplier and documented.

Explanation/what is required: Organizations must identify all the essential security controls and communicate to all employees/contractors/suppliers by creating a policy. Organizations need to mandate that suppliers adhere to the organizational policy and no unauthorized attempts be made for gaining access to the organization information and assets. It is important to define a clear procedure to implement identified security controls to guide the implementation teams.

An organization can consider the following points, while planning to manage supplier relationships.

- Identify and prepare the list of suppliers with information such as supplier name, type of services provided by the supplier for example services like IT, logistics, infrastructure, etc.

- Identify the types of access that need to be provided to all the different suppliers and how access will be monitored and controlled.

- Define the agreements with each supplier based on the information security control and business needs of the organization. Agreements must be signed by both parties i.e. by supplier and your organization, to ensure all the obligations arising out of the agreements are fulfilled by the supplier organization.

How will incident management be done, if any supplier related incidents occur. The organization must plan and conduct awareness sessions for members of the supplier's organization that would be accessing your organization's information and assets.

Evidence that can be prepared:

- Supplier relationship policy

- Agreement with suppliers

- List of users from supplier organization who have been given access

- Records of access permission monitoring to prevent information security breaches

198

Who prepares it:

- The information security team prepares the supplier relationship policy in discussion with various departments/implementation teams.

- The various department heads prepare the agreements based on the services acquired from each supplier.

- The IT Helpdesk team maintains a list of users from the supplier organization for access monitoring purposes.

For external audit: The external auditor conducting the ISO 27001 certification audit will check the policy/procedure/security controls/records in order to verify how organizations have implemented the security controls for preventing unauthorized access.

A.15.1.2 Addressing Security Within Supplier Agreements (ISO 27001 Control)

All relevant information security requirements should be established and agreed with each supplier that may access, process, store, communicate, or provide IT infrastructure components for the organization information.

Explanation/what is required: Once the supplier agreement is established between your organization and the supplier, both are aware of their obligations. This will also ensure that there are no misunderstandings between the organizations/parties. The agreement must be agreed and signed.

The following points could be considered for inclusion in the supplier agreement.

- Information that will be shared with the supplier organization and the methods to provide access to the information.

- Classification of information defined based on the classification scheme of your organization and the supplier.

- All the legal and statutory requirements, including the intellectual property rights, must be clearly mentioned.

Policies to be followed as required by the work scope and contract:

It is important to include that your organization has the right to audit supplier organization whenever there is a security incident, or any type of issue observed for investigation purposes.

There could be many more points that can be mentioned inside the agreement to avoid any conflicts between your organization and the supplier. These are just examples for reference purposes only. Organizations may add more depending on their business/ project scope.

Evidence that can be prepared:

- Supplier relationship policy

- Supplier agreement between your organization and the supplier

Who prepares it:

- The information security team prepares the supplier relationship policy in discussion with various departments/implementation teams.

- Concerned department heads prepare the agreements based on the services acquired from each supplier. Agreements must be reviewed by the legal team to avoid conflicts and legal issues in the future.

- The IT Helpdesk team maintains a list of users from the supplier organization for access monitoring purposes.

For external audit: The external auditor conducting the ISO 27001 certification audit will check the policy and the supplier agreement. To verify whether organizations have established the supplier agreement with the vendor/supplier, the agreement covers all the essential points to safeguard the organization's interests and avoid any conflicts, and whether the agreement was signed or expired will also be audited.

A.15.1.3 Information and Communication Technology Supply Chain (ISO 27001 Control)

Agreements with suppliers should include requirements to address the information security risks associated with information and communications technology services and product supply chain.

Explanation/what is required: The organization can include the following points in the supplier agreement for the provision of supply chain security into the products and services:

- The organization should clearly define the information security requirements for the information and communication technology product or services.

- Suppliers who are providing services along with subcontractors must ensure that they are responsible for complying to your organization's security requirements throughout the supply chain lifecycle.

- There should be procedures for monitoring and validating the products and services to ensure that they are adhering to defined/ agreed security requirements

- It is to be ensured that products and services that have been delivered will work as expected.

There could be many more points inside the agreement. These are just examples for reference purposes only. Organizations may add more depending on their business/ project scope.

Evidence that can be prepared:

- Supplier relationship policy

- Supplier agreement between your organization and the supplier

- Procedures for monitoring and validating products and services

- Results of monitoring and validating products and services

Who prepares it: The information security team prepares the supplier relationship policy in discussion with various departments/implementation teams.

Concerned department heads prepare the agreements based on the services acquired from each supplier. Agreements must be reviewed by the legal team to avoid any conflicts and legal issues in the future.

Concerned departments prepare the procedure and results for monitoring and validating products and services.

For external audit: The external auditor conducting the ISO 27001 certification audit will check the policy and the supplier agreement. To verify whether organizations have established the supplier agreement with the vendor/supplier, the agreement covers all the essential points to safeguard the products and services of supply chain.

A.15.2 Supplier Service Delivery Management

Objective: To maintain an agreed level of information security and service delivery in line with supplier agreements.

Explanation: Organizations must create the provisions to monitor and review the supplier service delivery performance based on the agreed security and service levels.

A.15.2.1 Monitoring and Review of Supplier Services (ISO 27001 Control)

Organizations should regularly monitor, review, and audit supplier service delivery.

Explanation/what is required: Once the supplier starts providing their services, they must be regularly monitored, reviewed, and audited.

Organizations can define the service management relationship procedure with the supplier to do the following:

- To monitor supplier required performance levels as per the agreed agreement terms.

- To review service reports produced by the supplier and conduct regular meetings as defined in the agreement.

- To conduct planned audits of the supplier processes and follow up on the closure of identified findings.

There could be many more points that can be mentioned for monitoring the performance of supplier performance. These points are for reference purposes only. Organizations may add more depending on their business/project scope

Evidence that can be prepared:

- Supplier relationship policy

- Supplier agreement covering the clause on monitoring and reviewing the supplier processes

- Service management relationship procedure

- Service reports shared by the supplier

- Results of monitoring, reviewing, and auditing activities

Who prepares it: The information security team prepares the supplier relationship policy in discussion with various departments/implementation teams.

Concerned department heads prepare the agreements based on the services acquired from each supplier. Agreements must be reviewed by the legal team to avoid any conflicts and legal issues in the future.

Concerned departments prepare the procedure and results for monitoring and validating products and services.

For external audit: The external auditor conducting the ISO 27001 certification audit will check the policy and the supplier agreement. They verify how monitoring, reviewing, and auditing activities have been performed by your organization and follow up on the closure of identified issues.

A.15.2.2 Managing Changes to Supplier Services (ISO 27001 Control)

Changes to the provision of services by suppliers, including maintaining and improving existing information security policies, procedures, and controls should be managed, considering of the criticality of business information, systems, and processes involved and re-assessment of risks.

Explanation/what is required: Once the supplier starts providing their services, changes to the services might be required. Once the agreement is revised, risk assessment must be done to identify the existence of new risks.

Organizations can consider the following scenarios:

- When you need to manage changes to the supplier agreements

- When you are proposing enhancements or modifications to the current system

- When you need to develop new systems.

When the supplier services change, it could be the following scenarios.

- When new products are developed or acquired

- You want to implement a new technology

- Any changes to office locations

- You want to change suppliers

Evidence that can be prepared:

- Supplier relationship policy

- Supplier agreement changes

- Revised/new agreement

- Risk assessment tracker

Who prepares it:

- The information security team prepares the supplier relationship policy in discussion with various departments/implementation teams.

- The concerned department heads revise or prepare new agreements based on the services acquired from each supplier. Agreements must be reviewed by the legal team to avoid any conflicts and legal issues in the future.

- The information security team assesses the new risks in discussion with the concerned department/stakeholder.

For external audit: The external auditor conducting the ISO 27001 certification audit will check the policy and the supplier agreement. They verify how supplier agreements are revised based on the organization's business needs. The risks are reassessed based on the changes.

A.16 Information Security Incident Management

A.16.1 Management of Information Security Incidents and Improvements

Objective: To ensure a consistent and effective approach to managing information security incidents, including communication on security events and weaknesses.

Explanation/what is required: Organizations must manage the incidents effectively by providing a timely response to them.

A.16.1.1 Responsibilities and Procedures (ISO 27001 Control)

Management responsibilities and procedures should be established to ensure a quick, effective, and orderly response to information security incidents.

Explanation/what is required: Management must ensure that incident management procedures are defined and communicated to all within the organization. Create a procedure to cover the following areas:

- How incident responses will be planned

- How incidents will be monitored, detected, analyzed, and reported in the organization

- How incident management activities will be logged

- How incidents will be assessed

- How incident escalation will be handled, recovery from an incident

- How incidents reporting will be done to report the security events and to plan the response actions.

- How incident details will be recorded—i.e. type of issue, messages appearing on screen, etc.—which could be shared with the incident response team for faster resolution

- How incident resolution status will be reported to the people who reported the incident and how feedback will be gathered about the incident resolution to confirm the result is acceptable and the incident status can be closed

It is important that skilled employees handle the response to the incidents to ensure that incidents are resolved in an effective manner.

Evidence that can be prepared:

- Incident management procedure

- Incident form/reports

- Incident resolution records/status

Who prepares it: The IT Helpdesk team can prepare all the evidence/records by consulting the information security team.

For external audit: The external auditor conducting the ISO 27001 certification audit will check the procedure/records to verify how the organization has defined and managed incident management activities, how incidents are reported, and the resolution status communicated with the incident reporter.

A.16.1.2 Reporting Information Security Events (ISO Control)

Information security events should be reported through appropriate management channels as quickly as possible.

Explanation/what is required: The requirement is whenever any employee or contractor observes any security events in the system, it must be reported to the incident response team as quickly as possible, so that they can respond to the incident faster to minimize its impact on the organization information security. It is important that employee/contractor must be made aware of the procedures for reporting the security events and knows to whom to report any security event.

Some of the scenarios could be considered security incidents. Organizations can assess and prepare their own security incident definitions.

- Incident due to human error/mistake

- Ineffective security controls

- Physical security access breaches

- Unauthorized/unapproved system changes

- Practices that are not followed as per policy and procedures

- Errors in the system i.e. software or hardware

Evidence that can be prepared:

- Incident management procedure

- Form/tools to report security events

- Records of training/awareness sessions to employees/contractors on incident reporting

Who prepares it: The IT Helpdesk team can prepare all the evidence/records by consulting the information security team.

For external audit: The external auditor conducting the ISO 27001 certification audit will check the procedure/records in order to verify how the organization has defined and managed incident management activities, how incidents are reported, and how the resolution status was communicated to the incident reporter.

A.16.1.3 Reporting Information Security Weaknesses (ISO Control)

Employees and contractors using the organization's information systems and services should be required to note and report any observed or suspected information security weaknesses in systems or services.

Explanation/what is required: Whenever any employee or contractor observes a security weaknesses in the system, they must report it to the incident response team as quickly as possible. It is important that the reporting mechanism be easy to use and readily available.

Evidence that can be prepared:

- Incident management procedure

- Form/tools to report security events

- Records of training/awareness sessions to employees/contractors on security weaknesses

Who prepares it: The IT Helpdesk team can prepare all the evidence/records by consulting the information security team.

For external audit: The external auditor conducting the ISO 27001 certification audit will check the procedure/records in order to verify how employee/contractors report the security weaknesses and what reporting mechanisms are provided.

A.16.1.4 Assessment of and Decision on Information Security Events (ISO Control)

Information security events should be assessed, and it should be decided if they are to be classified as information security incidents.

Explanation/what is required: Assess the information security event to decide whether the security event is really an information security incident, assessment to be done by the point of contact, incident response team by referring to the incident classification scale, as this will also help to assess the impact and priority of an incident. For future reference purposes, all the security events assessment results must be recorded.

Evidence that can be prepared:

- Incident management procedure

- Incident classification guideline

- Security events assessment results/records

Who prepares it: The IT Helpdesk team can prepare all the evidence/records by consulting the information security team.

For external audit: The external auditor conducting the ISO 27001 certification audit will check the procedure/records in order to verify how security events are assessed and classified as an information security incident. Also, they check how the details of the security events assessments results are recorded for future verification purposes.

A.16.1.5 Response to Information Security Incidents (ISO Control)

Information security events should be responded to in accordance with the documented procedures.

Explanation/what is required: The information security incident must be responded to by the designated member/point of contact of the organization. There could be scenarios where members from outside the organization need to respond to the security incident as well.

The following points should be included in the security incident response:

- Once the incident occurs, all possible evidence must be recorded.

- All the responses on the security incident must be logged, as it might be needed n the future for analysis purposes.

- Determine the root cause of the information security incident.

Once all the required actions are taken on the incident, the status should change to closed and all the details should be recorded.

Evidence that can be prepared:

- Incident management procedure

- Incident responses/results

Who prepares it: The IT Helpdesk team can prepare all the evidence/records by consulting the information security team.

For external audit: The external auditor conducting the ISO 27001 certification audit will check the procedure/records in order to verify how security incident responses are communicated and recorded by the organization.

A.16.1.6 Learning from Information Security Incidents (ISO Control)

Knowledge gained from analyzing and resolving information security should be used to reduce the likelihood or impact of future incidents.

Explanation/what is required: Organizations must analyze all the data collected during the evaluation of information security incident. This data will help to assess whether similar type of incidents may occur on a frequent basis. After the analysis of such data, organizations must identify appropriate security controls for implementation to minimize the occurrence and impact of information security incident. The whole purpose of this control is to plan and implement improvements.

Evidence that can be prepared:

- Incident management procedure

- Incident analysis/reports

Who prepares it: The IT Helpdesk team can prepare all the evidence/records by consulting the information security team.

For external audit: The external auditor conducting the ISO 27001 certification audit will check the procedure/records in order to verify how the security incident evaluation results are analyzed.

A.16.1.7 Collection of Evidence (ISO Control)

The organization should define and apply procedures for the identification, collection, acquisition, and preservation of information, all of which can serve as evidence.

Explanation/what is required: Organizations must create the provisions to protect and safely store the information that could serve as the potential evidence, which would be required whenever any disciplinary process is initiated. It is important that access to stored evidence must always be monitored, that they are not altered or deleted by unauthorized persons as they can hamper in the legal proceedings. Sometimes it becomes necessary that a lawyer or the police be involved as soon as possible.

Evidence that can be prepared:

- Incident management procedure

- Implemented security controls to protect the evidence

- List of people having access to the folders/files

- Regular reviews of access list/logs to monitor unauthorized access attempts made to the evidence folder/files

Who prepares it: The IT Helpdesk team can prepare all the evidence/records by consulting the information security team.

For external audit: The external auditor conducting the ISO 27001 certification audit will check the procedure/records in order to verify how security controls are implemented and monitored to protect the evidence from being altered or deleted.

A.17 Information Security Aspects of Business Continuity Management

A.17.1 Information Security Continuity

Objective: Information security continuity should be embedded in the organization's business continuity management systems.

Explanation/what is required: Protect information security from loss in any adverse situations that your organization may face. Organizations must always be prepared for adverse situations by establishing a robust business continuity management system.

A.17.1.1 Planning Information Security Continuity (ISO 27001 Control)

The organization should determine its requirements for information security and the continuity of information security management in adverse situations e.g. during a crisis or disaster.

Explanation/what is required: Perform robust planning for the organization's information security management in unexpected adverse situations. These situations are explained in earlier chapters—a fire, electricity/power blackout, floods, cyber-attack by a hacker. If there is no preparation/planning done, there could be big negative impact. Recovery from such situations could take a lot of time and money. It is therefore advisable that organizations conduct impact analysis on their business continuity requirements and plan for a strategy that will help them execute the disaster recovery plan quickly.

Evidence that can be prepared: Business impact analysis document. business continuity and disaster recovery policy.

Who prepares it: Information security would need to get input from various departments, including critical ones like the IT Helpdesk team, to conduct a business impact analysis and prepare a business continuity and disaster recovery policy.

For external audit: The external auditor conducting the ISO 27001 certification audit will check the business impact analysis and business continuity and disaster recovery policy. They verify how the organization has conducted the impact analysis to analyze all their critical business needs.

A.17.1.2 Implementing Information Security Continuity (ISO 27001 Control)

The organization should establish, document, implement, and maintain processes, procedures, and controls to ensure the required level of continuity for information security during an adverse situation.

Explanation/what is required: To face any adverse situation, the organization needs a lot of preparation. This includes approved documented plans, response and recovery procedures that explain the steps to be followed for different types of situations that may occur, and clear roles and responsibilities of employees/contractors/suppliers etc. with authorization levels to avoid miscommunicating. Preparing for business continuity is not a small task. It requires expertise with experienced skilled professionals who do a lot of analysis and planning. It is advisable that the organization identify their predetermined levels of information security they need to maintain after an adverse situation in order to run their business operations smoothly.

Evidence that can be prepared: Disaster response and recovery procedure and business continuity plan document

Who prepares it: Information security needs to get input from various departments including critical ones, such as the IT Helpdesk team, to prepare a business continuity and disaster recovery procedure and a business continuity plan document.

For external audit: The external auditor conducting the ISO 27001 certification audit will check the evidence in order to verify how the organization has done the planning and prepared their organization, i.e., what procedures will be followed by the teams to deal with adverse situations.

A.17.1.3 Verify, Review, and Evaluate Information Security Continuity (ISO 27001 Control)

The organization should verify the established and implemented information security continuity controls at regular intervals in order to ensure that they are valid and effective during adverse situations.

Explanation/what is required: Review and check whether there are any operational changes in the organization that require the business continuity planning and procedures to change.

For example, it is best to conduct a fire drill exercise for your organization/employees/emergency response teams as they would be aware and prepared to handle the situations effectively. During such situations, fire alarms should work, doors should be automatically open, water sprinklers must sprinkle water to douse the fire, and many more.

Wherever and whenever required, test your procedures, tools, technology, infrastructure etc. to ensure they are up to date, relevant, and would be enough to help your organization.

Evidence that can be prepared: Disaster response and recovery test procedure and test/review records

Who prepares it: the Information security, team along with the various departments stakeholders, will prepare test procedures and prepare test/review records after conducting various tests/reviews.

For external audit: The external auditor conducting the ISO 27001 certification audit will check the evidence in order to verify how the organization has identified relevant security controls and tested them to prepare for any adverse situations.

A.17.2 Redundancies

Objective: To ensure availability of information processing facilities.

Explanation: Ensure that systems and tools are available and working during adverse situations to support your company by establishing a robust business continuity management system.

A.17.2.1 Availability of Information Processing Facilities (ISO 27001 Control)

Information processing facilities should be implemented with redundancy enough to meet availability requirements.

Explanation/what is required: Ensure that during any adverse situations your organization's critical systems and tools are up and running to support the business operations. For example:

- If any critical IT server failure happens, a backup second server must be planned that should immediately take over and supports the applications. This failover will ensure that there is minimum information loss over a few seconds' switch time. The organization must analyze their business needs and determine which information/assets are critical.

- It is important that the organization test the servers in a planned manner to ensure the systems work as expected. Scenarios must be identified where availability of systems to safeguard information cannot be assured. Those must be identified as risks, to mitigate them in the future and communicate to management including all the stakeholders.

Evidence that can be prepared: Redundancy test planning, test records, and the risk tracker (for new risks identified during redundancy availability testing)

Who prepares it: The IT Helpdesk team, along with the information security team, will do redundancy test planning and prepare test records after conducting various tests. The risk tracker will be updated if there are new identified risks.

For external audit: The external auditor conducting the ISO 27001 certification audit will check the evidence in order to verify how the organization has identified relevant redundancy controls and tested them to prepare for any adverse situations.

A.18 Compliance

A.18.1 Compliance with Legal and Contractual Requirements

Objective: To avoid breaches of legal, statutory, regulatory, or contractual obligations related to information security and of any security requirements.

Explanation/what is required: Protect the organization by complying to legal and/ or obligations that are mentioned as part of the contract and agreement pertaining to information security requirements.

A.18.1.1 Identification of Applicable Legislation and Contractual Requirements (ISO 27001 Control)

All relevant legislative statutory, regulatory, and contractual requirements and the organization's approach to meet these requirements should be explicitly identified, documented, and kept up to date for each information system.

Explanation/what is required: Based on their business scope, an organization must identify and document all the applicable laws and contractual requirements that they need to comply to. Laws must be not only applicable to the country in which your organization is located, but also to the countries where your products and services will be sold, as well as from client and supplier perspective too. Whenever any changes happen in any laws or contractual obligations, organizations must identify and revise the relevant documents.

Evidence that can be prepared: Document covering all applicable laws, agreement/ contracts covering obligations, and the risk tracker (for new risks identified due to law or contractual obligations)

Who prepares it: Legal/law, the human resources team, and the information security team will identify and document all applicable laws and agreements/contracts covering obligations. The risk tracker will be updated if there are new identified risks.

For external audit: The external auditor conducting the ISO 27001 certification audit will check the evidence in order to verify how the organization has identified relevant laws and contractual obligations to avoid from legal breaches.

A.18.1.2 Intellectual Property Rights (ISO 27001 Control)

Appropriate procedures should be implemented to ensure compliance with legislative, regulatory, and contractual requirements related to intellectual property rights and use of proprietary software products.

Explanation/what is required: An organization must protect information/software/ tools/source code or any other material that could be considered intellectual property. Intellectual property protection is important because it is something created by your organization. If it is copied or stolen then it would be considered a breach of intellectual property rights.

It is something created by your client or supplier, but your organization is accessing/using it, so your organization must comply with all the laws and contractual obligations. Hence, your organization can create a documented procedure that can be followed to ensure compliance is always achieved. All the impacted teams/managers/stakeholders must be aware of all the legal and contractual obligations related to their departments, as failing to comply may result in legal penalties and impact the organization's image.

To protect intellectual property, the organization must analyze and identify security controls that are relevant to their business scope. Some examples to be considered are:

- Mention in the employment contract/letter that every employee must protect the organization's intellectual property rights

- In all the business/work agreements made with your client and suppliers

- All the purchased software/tools installed and used in your organization must be licensed and authorized for use. Always track the expiry of such license dates and renew them as required.

Evidence that can be prepared: Document policies and procedures for managing intellectual property, agreement/contracts, the risk tracker (for new risks identified due to legal or contractual obligations)

Who prepares it: Legal/law, the human resources team, and the information security team will identify and document evidence.

For external audit: The external auditor conducting the ISO 27001 certification audit will check the evidence in order to verify how the organization has identified and implemented security controls to protect intellectual property rights.

A.18.1.3 Protection of Records (ISO 27001 Control)

Records should be protected from loss, destruction, falsification, unauthorized access and unauthorized release, in accordance with legislative, regulatory, contractual, and business requirements.

Explanation/what is required: An organization must avoid breach of intellectual property rights. To do this, the organization must identify and implement all the required security controls.

Some of the examples that could be considered are:

- Create a data retention policy and procedure

- Define the data retention period for each type of information/data/record

- Define how the data is stored i.e. paper/files/electronic media

- Define how access is managed to the stored information

- After the data retention period is over, how will the data be disposed of.

Evidence that can be prepared: Data retention policy and procedure, tools/files where data is stored, list of people with access, and review of access permissions

Who prepares it: Department heads/managers along with the information security team will identify and document evidence.

For external audit: The external auditor conducting the ISO 27001 certification audit will check the evidence in order to verify how the organization has identified and implemented security controls for the protection of records.

A.18.1.4 Privacy and Protection of Personally Identifiable Information (ISO 27001 Control)

Privacy and protection of personally identifiable information should be ensured as required in relevant legislations and regulations where applicable.

Explanation/what is required: An organization must create the provisions to safeguard the personally identifiable information of employees/contractors/clients/users/suppliers, etc. The organization must be aware of personally identifiable information i.e. personal identification number, credit card details, health information, etc. It is very important that organizations get consent from all employees/contractors/clients/users/suppliers before storing their personal information for official purposes. The organization can define a procedure to explain how this information will be stored and protected from unauthorized access. All stakeholders must understand their roles and responsibilities and the importance of safeguarding such information.

Some of the examples that could be considered are:

- Create policies and procedures for stakeholders to follow.

- The human resources team can get the written consent from employees/contractors to store their information. The form should mention the information details that will be stored, for how many years, and the purpose of storing.

- The organization can also put the request message on their company websites for the site visitors to inform them for capturing their cookies information and providing them with the options to either accept or reject this request. Also, for any form that's filled in online on your organization website and is storing personal information, you must get consent.

- Get consent from clients and suppliers via contracts/agreements.

- Put controls to protect this stored information.

- Define how users make requests to your organization to delete their personal information.

- After the data retention period is over, define how you dispose of the personal information.

Evidence that can be prepared: Protection of personally identifiable information policy and procedures, consent evidence i.e. via paper forms signed or online application acceptances, list of people with access to the information, review of access permissions, users request records to delete their personal information, and information disposal evidence

Who prepares it: Department heads/managers along with the information security team will identify and document evidence.

For external audit: The external auditor conducting the ISO 27001 certification audit will check the evidence in order to verify how the organization identified and implemented security controls for the privacy and protection of personal identifiable information.

A.18.1.5 Regulation of Cryptography Controls (ISO 27001 Control)

Cryptographic controls should be used in compliance with all relevant agreements, legislation, and regulations.

Explanation/what is required: An organization must use the cryptographic controls in compliance with all relevant agreements, legislation, and regulations, as there could be restrictions on the way it needs to be implemented. Failure to comply may result in fines or could impact the company image. Hence, organizations are advised to discuss with their legal team to analyze the specific legal requirements in countries where they are operate.

Evidence that can be prepared: Cryptography usage policy and evidence of cryptography usage

Who prepares it: Department heads/managers along with the information security team will identify and document evidence.

For external audit: The external auditor conducting the ISO 27001 certification audit will check the evidence in order to verify how the organization has identified and implemented cryptographic controls.

A.18.2 Information Security Reviews

Objective: To ensure that information security is implemented and operated in accordance with the organizational policies and procedures.

Explanation: The organization must ensure that they have implemented information security by following their defined policies and procedures.

A.18.2.1 independent Review of Information Security (ISO 27001 Control)

The organization's approach to managing and implementing information security (i.e., control objectives, controls, policies, processes, and procedures for information security) should be reviewed independently at planned intervals or when significant changes occur.

Explanation/what is required: The requirement is that an organization must plan independent reviews at regular intervals, which are driven by management. This is to ensure that implemented information security management system—the policies, procedures, and security controls—are compliant and suitable for use. Wherever there are improvements identified and changes needed, they must be promptly implemented.

If these reviews are conducted by internal teams, the reviewer/auditor must be from a of different area or department so that there is no bias while conducting the review. The review could also be conducted by an external agency. The identified reviewer must be skilled and experienced. Results of these reviews must be presented to management for their awareness and to seek any feedback. When non-compliance is identified, proper corrective actions must be identified to fix it.

Evidence that can be prepared

- Review/audit plan

- Reviewer/auditor list

- Training records of reviewer/auditor list

- Results of review/audit

Who prepares it: The information security team is responsible for reviewing security along with the relevant stakeholders.

For external audit: The external auditor conducting the ISO 27001 audit may check for all the stated evidence.

Summary

This chapter covered how to implement the ISO 27001 control by adopting the 27002 guidelines shared by the standard. Then you learned about all the information security controls that you need to implement and execute in your organization in order to make your system audit ready and to successfully complete the ISMS audit.

References

This chapter is based on the practical tips of the author while implementing various controls and from the ISO/IEC 27001 and 27002 standard guidelines, also known as "Security Techniques: Code of Practice for Information Security Controls".

CHAPTER 7

Internal Audit

"An active and informed audit committee provides the ultimate independent and objective oversight of the corporate control environment, including a focus on emerging trends and risks. Internal auditing is the primary agent of the audit committee within the company."

—Ford Motor Company

The previous chapter discussed implementing security controls as per the ISO 27001 standard guide. You also learned about the need for policies and procedures required during the implementation process.

This chapter focuses on understanding the internal audit requirements, conducting the audit, preparing the audit report, and closing the findings before the external audit. This chapter lays the foundation for the following:

- Preparing an internal audit team

- Conducting audits

- Closing findings/gaps

- Planning improvement

- Communicating

Preparing an Internal Audit Team

Once all the security control implementation is done, it's time to perform an internal audit to verify the accuracy of the implementation and to ensure that no more gaps exist.

© Abhishek Chopra, Mukund Chaudhary 2020
A. Chopra and M. Chaudhary, *Implementing an Information Security Management System*,
https://doi.org/10.1007/978-1-4842-5413-4_7

The information security team may form an audit team by selecting experienced members or subject matter experts from relevant departments who will be responsible for identifying and closing gaps. Choosing an internal auditor can be a strategic decision for the organization.

The audit team should include people from different departments, such as the IT department, software development, human resources, and the finance department. To make them part of the ISO 27001 audit team, they need to take an internal auditor or ISO lead implementer training course, which will teach them how to plan, execute, and report on an ISMS audit.

Once the audit team is prepared, they undergo training, which helps them understand the current standards knowledge, which in turns expands their existing knowledge and skills and makes them qualified to conduct an internal audit. The core focus of training the audit team is to make them prepared for the audit.

Some companies identify an experienced person within the organization to perform the internal audit, while other companies use an external auditor.

Here are a few of the types of internal auditor that an organization needs:

- *Full-time internal auditor:* Organization whose scope of work is very large and that have more audit work prefer a full-time resource. For example, banks need to obey the law and have such roles.

- *Part-time internal auditor:* This is the most common case in small or mid-sized organizations. These types of organizations prefer someone who will perform his regular job throughout the year and conduct an internal audit several times as per the requirements.

- *Internal auditor from outside the organization:* Some companies prefer a person from outside the organization to conduct the internal audit. This may be due to lack of skill within the organization or due to limited resources. It is important to note that the consultant or expert will be allowed to do the audit as per the organization policy only.

Note   It is best to have at least two auditors so that they can audit each other's work to avoid any conflict of interest.

What are the characteristics you should look before hiring an outside consultant?

The answer is very simple—hire a consultant who can add value to the organization, who matches your requirements, and who can reduce your implementation time by providing solutions or alternative ways.

Some of the parameters that companies keep in mind when hiring a third-party consultant or internal auditor are as follows:

- *Experience of auditor:* It should be obvious that when you're hiring a consultant for your ISO 27001 internal audit, you should look at the experience level and expertise of the consultant. Consider asking a few questions:

  - How many years of experience do you have with ISO 27001 implementation/auditing?

  - Are you a certified ISO 27001 lead implementer or ISO 27001 lead auditor (or have any other certificate that indicates you are trained for this job)?

  - In which industry do you have the most experience? For example, an auditor must have domain understanding. If an auditor is from an IT background and has no experience with the banking domain, he's not a good choice for a banking audit.

- *Regional auditor:* When you are hiring an auditor, it is very important that she knows your language in order to communicate effectively. Also, when the auditor is from the same region, traveling is not a challenge.

- *Reputation:* It is very important to take services from well-recognized vendors or consultants. If this subject matter expert has published articles or books, for example, chances are you are hiring the correct person.

Tip   Watch out for consultants who focus more on selling their tools and materials rather than understanding your business requirements.

Conducting Audits

When you choose to implement ISO 27001 ISMS, you are required to conduct an internal audit.

The ISO 27001 internal audit helps you examine whether your organization-defined ISMS is compliant with the standard requirements. It also helps the organization achieve its set business objectives and ensures that the organizational policy and procedures you've implemented are being followed.

Auditing is time consuming and requires the organization to work on the process improvement part continuously. The frequency of the internal audit varies depending on the organization's need and the complexity of the system or process they are following. Generally, organizations plan for semiannual internal audits.

If an organization recognizes multiple risks, they could perform internal audit more frequently. The banking system, for example, requires a regular internal auditor. Most organizations are free to choose the frequency of their internal audits—monthly, quarterly, semiannually, or yearly.

Note   All ISO management system standards (such as ISO 9001, ISO 14001, and ISO 27001) require the organization to conduct a regular internal audit as part of its performance evaluation.

Audit Plan

Whenever you do some important activity in your life, it's a good idea to plan for it first. For example, when you go on vacation, you plan the travel, and then plan for the stay. Why do we plan in this manner? The answer is to avoid any risk during your vacation or trip.

Similarly, when you audit your organization, planning is a must. Before initializing the internal audit, the organization must develop an audit plan that defines the audit's objectives, scope, and criteria. The following key items cover what you should take care of when planning for an ISO 27001 internal audit:

1. *Objective and scope of audit plan:* The client should define the objectives and scope of the audit. Here are some examples of good objectives:

   - To assess the implementation and effectiveness of the ISO 27001 controls.

   - To assess compliance with the applicable laws and regulations.

   - To assess compliance with internal policies and procedures.

   Similarly, the scope should also be covered in the audit plan. For example; the scope of work for internal audit can be:

   - To review the policies and procedures of the organization.

   - To review the means of safeguarding assets of the organization.

   - To review the laws and regulations that impact the business.

   The scope of the audit should include a description of the physical location of the organization, units, support functions, and any exclusions.

2. *Audit schedule:* Once the scope of the audit is clear, the next thing to do is to prepare the audit schedule. The audit schedule will cover all the projects/departments that will be audited as part of the new audit cycle. It is also important to share the audit schedule with the auditor/auditees and the management team, as full commitment is needed from every stakeholder during this exercise. Even with an external audit, the lead auditor will verify the audit schedule as evidence of an organization's commitment to the internal audit exercise. This schedule usually includes the location of the audit, the start date, the end date, and the name of the auditor/auditees.

Note   Recently closed projects are not typically included but can be included to check the whole process and to learn how security controls are planned and implemented during this project's lifecycle. If specific feedback needs to be shared with the team members, it will be helpful for the future projects.

Figure 7-1 shows a sample audit schedule.

				Internal Audit Plan					
SI #	Project/Departm ent Name	Name of Auditor	Name of Auditees	Audit Scope	Date	Time	Actual Date and Time	Remarks
1	Project ABC			Project Management & Engineering Practices				
2	Project XYZ			Project Management & Engineering Practices				
3	HR & Recruitment			HR operations				
4	IT Helpdesk			IT operations				
5	Training			Training operations				
6	Procurement			Procurement operations				

Figure 7-1. *An internal audit sample plan*

3. *Audit teams:* The audit team consists of the auditor (the one who audits the organization to achieve the business objective) and the auditees (ones being audited). For example, the departments such as HR, IT, finance, and other support functions who take part in the audit could be the auditees.

Pre-Audit Meeting/Briefing

There can be one or more pre-audit meeting between the information security team and the auditors. It should take place no later than one day before the actual audit. The objectives of the meeting should include:

- Ensure the availability of all the resources needed and other logistics that may be required by the auditor.

- Verify the scope of the audit from the audit plan.

Opening Meeting

The opening meeting is conducted on the day of the audit, but before the start of the actual audit. The auditee/auditors, CISO (Chief Information Security Officer), and senior management may participate. The purpose of the opening meeting is to brief the team about the objective of this audit. The following topics should be discussed during the meeting:

- Describe the purpose and scope of the audit to the team.

- Present the confirmation of the audit plan.

- Discuss the general guidelines/rules to be followed by the audit team during the audit.

It's now time to discuss how to conduct the audit. Audits are generally conducted using an audit checklist. A checklist is a suitable means of performing an internal audit, as checking each control one by one will ensure that you have not missed any controls and you can meet the audit requirements.

Figure 7-2 shows the sample HR audit checklist. Similarly, you can have a checklist for all the departments as part of the ISMS audit.

HR Audit Checklist

#	Questions	Status (Yes/No/NA)	Remarks
	ISO 27001 Audit Questions		
1	Are you following the joining, shifting and exit formalities? Is there any documented procedure?		
2	Can you show the evidence for this process?		
3	Have your team undergone ISMS Trainings?		
4	How frequently you will conduct ISMS awareness training		
5	What security objectives are communicated and how, what actions were taken, etc., within the team ?		
6	Understand how the sources of non-conformity are identified and monitored. Violations, breaches, audit findings, non-compliance notices, etc., may lead to non-		
7	Does all employees have signed the NDA?		
8	Does all employees have signed employment contract?		
9	How do you ensure that third parties / contractors are aware of their information security responsibilities? (for		
10	Have you identified the risks related to HR department? How these risks have been addressed?		
12	Have you classified and labelled all documents related to Human resource?		

Figure 7-2. *A sample audit checklist for the HR department*

You can start your audit with a document review, which includes checking the policy and procedure documents. Some mandatory documents must be produced to the auditor to be ISO 27001 compliant. The list of documents is as follows:

- Scope of the ISMS—This is as per Clause 4.3.

- Information security policy and objectives—As per Clauses 5.2 and 6.2.

- Risk assessment and risk treatment methodology—Per Clause 6.1.2.

- Statement of Applicability—Per Clause 6.1.3d

- Risk treatment plan—This is mandatory per Clauses 6.1.3e and 6.2.

- Risk assessment report—Per Clause 8.2.

- Definition of security roles and responsibilities—The roles and responsibilities should be clearly defined for the ISMS audit. This gives everyone a clear understanding of the expectations from the different teams and is mandatory as per Clauses A.7.1.2 and A.13.2.4.

- Inventory of assets—Mandatory as per Clause A.8.1.1.

- Acceptable use of assets—As per Clause A.8.1.3.

- Access control policy—As per Clause A.9.1.1.

- Operating procedures for IT management - This is again one of the important clauses A.12.1.1.

- Secure system engineering principles—As per Clause A.14.2.5.

- Supplier security policy—Clause A.15.1.1.

- Incident management procedure—This is again very important if you are doing ISMS to reduce your incidents and is mandatory per Clause A.16.1.5.

- Business continuity procedures—Business continuity is crucial and it is recommended to read ISO 22301 (the business continuity management system). BCP is mandatory as per Clause A.17.1.2.

- Statutory, regulatory, and contractual requirements—As per Clause A.18.1.1.

You also need to check these mandatory records:

- Training records, skills, experience, and qualifications—As per Clause 7.2.

- Regular monitoring and measurement results—As per Clause 9.1.

- Internal audit program—As per Clause 9.2.

- Recording results of internal audits—As per Clause 9.2.

- Results of the management review—As per Clause 9.3.

- Record the result of corrective actions—As per Clause 10.1.

- Logs of all user activities, exceptions, and security events—As per Clauses A.12.4.1 and A.12.4.3.

Note   To perform the audit, you need to meet relevant departments, review their processes and procedures, and sometimes physically verify the controls.

Audit's Finding Report

Once the audit is completed, the internal auditor must present the audit's finding report to the auditees. The audit's finding report must clearly define the weakness or risks identified. You may include the following sections in your audit report:

- Introduction to the audit scope, objectives, and methodology used for conducting an audit.

- Summary of key findings of the weaknesses or non-compliance areas.

- Recommendations and suggestion on any given control. It is purely the auditees' choice whether to accept or reject the suggestions shared by the auditor.

As shown in Figure 7-3, the internal audit report covers the following items:

- The sample report contains any non-conformities observed during the auditor's interaction with the auditees or during the document review.

- The root cause is where the auditor indicates why the issue or non-conformity occurs.

- The report also contains corrective or the preventive actions that need to be taken by the auditees during the closure of the gaps/ findings.

Sr. No	Audit Type	Auditor's Details	Audit Start Date (dd/mm/yy)	Standard	Clause / domain / Control Objectives	Category of Finding (NC/ Observation)	Description and Consequence
1	Internal Audit	Empanelled consultant		ISO 27001	A.11.3.3	NC	Although the Clear Desk & Clear Screen Policy is documented but few desk were found to be
2	Internal Audit	Empanelled consultant		ISO 27001	A.9.1.1	NC	No visitor cards issued to the visitors

Columns to be in Continuation, Shown for illustration only

Process / Area / Department / Location if multsite	Root Cause	Corrective Action to Prevent Recurrence	Preventive Action	Deadline for Implementation of Corrective Action (dd/mm/yy)	Date for Closure of Non-Conformity (dd/mm/yy)	Remarks
	Due to lack of awareness of Policy.	Admin Head was given direction to remove the paper & store them in safe place, and clear	The Admin Head read the Policy & ensured policy is read by his sub-ordinates.			Put your remark here.
	Due to lack of awareness of Policy by the security guard	admin Head has been given instruction to ensure the policy is implemented	The required training for the awareness of ISO 27001 will be given in order to ensure smooth working of all the			Awareness related to all policies and procedures have been imparted tc the ISMS

Figure 7-3. *The sample audit report*

Closing the Findings and Gaps

After conducting the audit and sharing the report with the auditees, it is important to close the findings. Auditees must reply to the findings reported in their areas by filling out the corrective and preventive action summary shown in Figure 7-2. *Corrective actions* refer to immediate actions that the team will take to close the information security gaps. *Preventive actions* refer to the steps or processes the team needs to address so that these security gaps do not occur again.

To close the finding, you need to revisit your finding report and understand the weakness or non-compliance. By reading the recommended strategy mentioned by the auditor, you can easily close them.

For example, say the auditor gave you non-compliance (NC) in Control A.11.3.3, which says you must have a clear desk and screen policy. First look at the description of this finding. In this example shown in Figure 7-2, the finding says that "Although the clear desk and clear screen policy is documented, a few desks were found to be cluttered with loose papers, files, and folders on the desktop screen."

This is clearly a non-compliance case. The team responsible for this compliance needs to know the root cause of this NC. The example says that it was due to lack of awareness. So, in order to resolve this non-compliance, you need to make the team aware of the rule and take actions to resolve it. The department head can be directed to remove the papers from the desk and instructed to store them in a safe place. The team can also be advised to read the policy document again and follow it.

By following these generic steps for all the non-compliances or weaknesses, you can close the gaps. The auditor can then review the changes to ensure that the list of weakness or gaps no longer exists.

Planning Improvement

Once you complete the audit findings, it becomes important to assess where your information security implementation is weak. For some organizations, this can be their first implementation exercise or their first internal audit exercise. In general, it is assumed and expected that in the first implementation, all the improvement areas cannot be implemented. You know there could be constraints and challenges at various levels in your organization or office site, etc.

Also, once you look closely at findings that were observed during the internal audit, you might see the various reasons that they impacted the implementation.

Here are the sample examples, which could be the possible reasons for the gaps:

1. Lack of awareness.

2. Half implementation only.

   • Policy doesn't cover all scope areas.

   • All the controls in policy were not fully implemented.

3. The wrong implementation.

4. Practice not followed consistently. For example, access rights reviews are not performed periodically.

5. New areas not discovered during the planning stage may remain uncovered.

When you look at these points, it will give you an overall picture that you might have to improve. If you don't want to improve them, what can happen? If you allow the gaps to remain in the system, they will grow further and create new problems. You cannot predict the impact of the new problems unless and until you are aware of the actual root causes. Hence, it is important to eliminate these gaps from the system as early as possible.

Eliminating Gaps

Now it's time to prepare an action plan for the identified improvements and gaps. You need to list all the identified areas for improvement, in the order of largest impact to least impact. The goal is to eliminate big problems first. Okay, so it may not be possible to execute all large impact improvements first. At the same time, it is important to update management, so that they are aware and informed about such improvements/decisions.

Once the improvement list is set, assign the owner and the timeline for each improvements. It is important to give them enough time (realistically) for each improvement. The improvements must be planned effectively and, once implemented, they must give the desired result. Hence, it is important to track the progress of the implemented improvements. This is the responsibility of the information security team, as the improvement tracker is their job. Any deviation and progress must be tracked so that planned improvements are completed with less deviation in the schedule. If you read all these points, you'll see that they follow the PDCA (Plan, Do, Check, and Act) cycle. PDCA is *the* essence of all ISO standards.

Can You Eliminate All Gaps?

With the limited resources/facilities that most people work under these days, it might not be feasible to eliminate all the gaps. In such scenarios, you usually can't work on the gaps together or in parallel.

Trying to eliminate all the gaps might not be as effective, as the desired result may lack quality. Most improvements need to be incorporated by teams/employees. If you try to implement an improvement without team buy-in, it won't be accepted by the team, which would defeat the purpose.

Communicating

During the ISO 27001 implementation, it is very important to communicate at every stage. During the internal audit process, it becomes important to communicate with everyone as well.

So, why is it so important to communicate?

One thing that most organizations lack is good communication within the organization and with the employees. During the audit process, not every employee gets audited. A few representatives from the team will face the audit team's questions. It is not feasible to audit each employee, as auditing is a sampling exercise.

When many members are not involved, it becomes important to communicate the status and findings noted during the audit to all the employees in the organization. People are the most important factor in information security breaches. Hence, it is important to keep the people in the organization updated about the security findings and their associated impacts. This will help reduce security incidents in the organization.

Note   The audit team can create a communication plan along with the audit plan. This will not only boost the team's communication but will also ensure that nothing is missed because of poor coordination or different communication styles.

Summary

In this chapter, you learned about the importance of the internal audit. It must be performed as part of the implementation exercise and is a mandatory part of the ISO 27001 standard. You also learned what's covered as part of the audit process. For example, you must form audit teams, perform audit training, set up an audit schedule, create the audit report, and close any gaps. The chapter also explained the importance of preparing and executing the improvement plan to further strengthen your organization's ISMS.

CHAPTER 8

Management Review

"The best way to get management excited about a disaster plan is to burn down the building across the street."

—Dan Erwin

This chapter explains how to plan and conduct the management review meeting and which aspects need to be taken into consideration while conducting this review. This chapter covers the following topics:

- Conducting the review

- Planning for improvements

- Communicating

Conducting the Review

When you implement large improvement initiatives in an organization, it is essential for management to know about them. And this is also a requirement of the ISO 27001 standard. Organizations must plan and conduct the standard based on a frequency that's feasible to the organization.

Organizations, at a minimum, should plan for semiannual management review meetings. The decisions made at such meetings are made for the future improvement of the organization and their impacts/benefits can usually be analyzed in a six-month timeframe. This way, the organization does not have to wait too long to know the benefits achieved from a previous plan or course of action. Also, if any planned initiatives/decisions aren't working, changes can be made accordingly. Hence, this is the reason that the ISO 27001 standard clearly requires management commitment. It's critical to improving the ISMS implemented in the organization/business unit.

© Abhishek Chopra, Mukund Chaudhary 2020
A. Chopra and M. Chaudhary, *Implementing an Information Security Management System*,
https://doi.org/10.1007/978-1-4842-5413-4_8

What Is Expected from Department Heads/Stakeholders?

As mentioned, a lot of time is required from the department heads and their teams, as they need to collect and analyze the data in order to prepare the presentation. They report on the security controls that are working, what is yet to be implemented, and issues that need discussion from management to arrive at the conclusion.

The data that's collected are the information security objectives/KPIs from each department. The KPIs/metrics performance achieved in the past month or on a monthly basis show whether you are achieving the information security objectives. This will show management that teams are following the processes needed to maintain the ISMS.

It is true that department heads/teams collect that data for analysis on a monthly basis and then share that information with middle management as part of their monthly review meetings.

However, in order to meet the defined information security objectives, it's better to observe performance over a longer period, such as quarterly, semiannually, or yearly. Only then can you conclude that the performance you want is achieved consistently (i.e., the security controls are working fine over time).

Therefore, you can see why it's better to conduct a management review meeting on a semiannual basis and not on a monthly basis.

Scheduling the Management Review Meeting

You can schedule this meeting in two ways.

First Way

If an organization is trying to implement the ISMS the first time, it is best to schedule the review meeting after all the policies and procedures are defined, the security controls are implemented, and one round of the internal audit exercise has been completed.

Note   Sometimes it is not feasible to implement all the controls before the first review. In such scenarios, you don't have to wait. You can go ahead with the review meeting to discuss what is implemented. You should always ensure whatever is implemented has been audited once.

Second Way

In some organizations, the implementation has been complete for a year or two, but they never planned the management review meeting. Such organizations must plan for the review and, once the first management review is conducted, a second management review should be planned in six months. This way, the management reviews are conducted in a planned manner. This is the best way for an organization that has already secured ISO 27001 certification and is now maintaining it.

Schedule the Meeting

Look for a suitable day to schedule the management review meeting, ensuring that all members can attend. Send the invite to all the participants/stakeholders at least two weeks in advance so that they can mark their calendars and have enough time to prepare. Otherwise, participants might feel that they don't time to prepare and nobody wants to go in front of management unprepared.

Preparing the Presentation

The easiest way to present the data is to prepare a slideshow presentation. The information security team should prepare a common template, which will be helpful for all the participants to follow. When all participants prepare their presentation in their own formats, it takes participants more time to understand and there is a chance that important points regarding security controls might get missed. Using a predefined common format is advisable. If there are specific points that need to be part of the format, they can always be added (the information security team should clarify this when sharing the presentation format.)

Tip   Department heads should share the presentations with the information security team so they can review them before they are finalized.

The information security team also has to prepare a presentation to showcase the areas that they are responsibility for. They should also highlight any issues/challenges they are facing that need to be discussed during the review meeting.

Items To Be Covered in the Presentation

From the information security team:

- Information security policy—Discuss if any changes are required in the policy statement or whether it is okay as is.

- Organization risks and opportunities—Discuss the risks that are critical, actions taken to address them, and the risks for which action is still pending.

- Information security objectives—Discuss the status of the defined objectives, whether you're meeting them or not, any challenges, etc.

- Resource status—Discuss critical tools or any manpower needed or any other requirements related to resources.

- Internal audit findings—Discuss the total findings observed in the internal audit, the status of the findings, their corrective/preventive actions, whether all findings are closed, and the challenges in closing them.

- ISMS implementation status—Organizations that have implemented ISMS for the first time should discuss the status of implementation and cover any challenges in achieving the objective.

- Process improvements implemented—Mention observed improvements. Management wants to see such improvements, so they can see that the ISMS implementation is improving the organization's information security system.

Tip There should not be any last-minute surprises/scenarios that crop up. Management will expect the teams to come with solutions to any problems they found. When you are discussing a problem with management, it is always advisable to suggest a few solutions.

From other departments:

- Department risks and opportunities—Discuss the critical risks, the actions taken to address them, and the actions that are still pending due to constraints or challenges.

- Department KPI—Discuss the status of the defined KPI, whether it's meeting or not, any challenges etc.

- Change in policy or procedure—If there have been changes, they should be shared in the review meeting.

By covering these points in the presentation, you can have better discussion/presentation during the review meeting. Apart from the presentation, you should also prepare for the questions that management might ask. If you cannot answer or do not have any supporting data available, it can be awkward to handle at the time.

Hence, it is best to be prepared and aware about what questions they might ask. This will help you during the review meeting.

Conducting the Review Meeting

On the day of the meeting, you can start the session with the information security team. The CISO or information security manager can review the agenda of the meeting and then continue to present the points, as mentioned in this chapter. After the information security team speaks, each department head can then present her own ISMS status.

The meeting can be conducted either by inviting all participants/department heads or stakeholders together at the same time, or they can be given an individual timeslot, and according to this timeslot, participants arrive and give their presentations. This scenario can work if you don't need all the participants to be present at the same time, or simply cannot find a time where they can all come.

It is more beneficial to conduct the meeting with all department heads present, as this way, the important points discussed can be shared with all parties at the same time. These critical issues could very well be of importance to these department heads. Also, if management wants to convey an important message during the meeting, it can be done easily with all affected parties present.

Here are some important points to remember during the review meeting:

- As part of the review meeting, you are presenting the organization's performance in implementing and managing the ISMS and not an individual employees' performances. Hence, you should never pinpoint any one person or department with fault.

- The data/values you present must be absolutely correct. Any error in the data can cause management to lose confidence in the process; hence, all the data should be reviewed thoroughly.

After completing the presentation, the CISO from the information security team should communicate to all the participants the action points that were developed during the review meeting and get their commitment to close them by the agreed-upon timeline.

Note   If any commitment is required from the management/steering committee during the review meeting, it should be acknowledged at this same time. It is difficult to get commitments later, and you may not have the opportunity to bring them all together again soon.

After the meeting session, it is important to prepare the meeting minutes by covering the following:

- Participants' names
- Meeting agenda
- Points discussed
- Action items, with owners and target dates

The meeting's minutes should be circulated/shared with all the participants, including senior management, on the same day or the day after the meeting.

Figure 8-1 shows a snapshot of some example ISMS meeting minutes. For better understanding, the agenda is filled in and the rest are blank.

MEETING:	ISO 27001 / ISMS Management Review Meeting

Name	Title	Present	Name	Title	Present

DATE, TIME, PLACE:

Date	Time	Place

ROLES:

Chair	Facilitator	Minute Taker	Documenter

Agenda	Actions / Decisions Taken	Action Owner	Target Closure Date
1. Presentation of Management Review Agenda and Minutes a. Status of Actions from Previous Management Reviews			
b. Strategic Direction			
▪ Internal Issues			
▪ External Issues			
c. Management Review Agenda ▪ Nonconformities and Corrective Actions			
▪ Security Objective, Targets Monitoring and Measurement Results			
▪ Internal Audit Results			
▪ Issues on/with External Providers / Interested Parties			
▪ Adequacy of Resources			
d. Effectiveness of Actions in Addressing Risks / Opportunities			
2. Identification of Continual Improvement Actions a. Continual Improvement Opportunities			
b. Changes needed to the ISMS			
3. ISMS Implementation status			
4. Other Matters			
5. Closing			

Figure 8-1. *Sample snapshot of meeting minutes*

Plan Improvement

If you refer to the meeting minutes that were prepared after the review meeting, they should cover all the improvement initiatives. Each action item can be taken as one improvement or broken into multiple improvements. One of the important goals of the review meeting is to find any improvement areas. Just imagine all the department heads together identifying improvement areas at the same time. This can also be considered a brainstorming exercise.

All these improvement areas should be mentioned and tracked as part of the improvement plan/tracker as well.

What Do You Improve?

You improve the following:

- Business processes and efficiency

- Security objectives/KPIs

- Awareness of the employees

- Overall effectiveness of the organization's ISMS

How Do You Know if You Have Improved?

This is an important question. Management needs to be able to see how the organization has improved. The information security team needs to track the status of each improvement initiative and collect the data to analyze the progress. As part of this, you must compare previous data with data after the implementation and determine whether improvements have been made or not. You also need to determine the scope and size of the improvements.

You need to keep collecting data on a monthly basis. When the time comes for the next management review meeting, you must present this data to management. This way, you manage the ISMS improvement on a year-over-year basis.

Communicate

Here, the information security team and the other department heads must communicate with each other on a regular basis about the status of the improvement areas. If it's clear that, after the management review meeting, there is no follow-up or communication on the action items noted during the review meeting, this will start impacting the momentum of the ISMS management initiatives.

If the information security team stops following up with the owners/department heads, the people in charge of the action items might not work on them. They might not see these items as their direct charge, and this could delay the initiative target date unnecessarily.

If no significant improvements are made then, during the next management review meeting, management will take notice. They might ask why you have not made any progress. This could be difficult to explain if you did not get support from the action item owners or the information security department could not complete the work.

Hence, it is advisable to track the status of all the action items on the semiweekly or monthly basis. This way, you'll know whether you are on the right track and progressing well or not. If things are not moving, you can follow up in a timely manner and even escalate things to management. Recall that, during the management review meeting, every member gave their commitment to providing support to the improvement initiatives.

Summary

This chapter taught you the importance of conducting a management review and gave you practical tips on how to conduct it. You also learned about improvement plans and how to track the plan with the team. You lastly learned about the importance of communicating progress and updates with all stakeholders.

CHAPTER 9

External Audit

"Uncontrolled access to data, with no audit trail of activity and no oversight, would be going too far. This applies to both commercial and government use of data about people."

—John Poindexter

This chapter covers external audits, which is the last stage of your ISO 27001 implementation. This chapter also explains the external audit requirements, including how to prepare for an audit, the best practices to manage the audit, and closing an audit. The chapter covers the following topics:

- Audit preparation
- Best practices
- Audit closure

Audit Preparation

After spending several months on the ISMS implementation, your teams are progressing toward the final stage of the implementation, which is the certification audit.

Note For organizations that do not want to go through the certification audit, the internal audit is considered the last stage of their first ISMS implementation.

It's not really the last stage, as your focus should be to aim for the continual improvement in the implementation of the ISMS.

© Abhishek Chopra, Mukund Chaudhary 2020
A. Chopra and M. Chaudhary, *Implementing an Information Security Management System*,
https://doi.org/10.1007/978-1-4842-5413-4_9

Before you move to the external audit phase, it is important to be sure the team is prepared. Facing an audit without being prepared will lead to failure. Time spent preparation is worth every second, as it will give your team confidence and make them audit-ready.

An external ISO 27001 audit can be eventful if you are new to the management standard framework. The good news is that it is structured in such a manner that beginners and small organization/business can be audited with ease.

An external audit in ISO 27001 can be divided into three stages, all of which are discussed in the following sections.

Stage 1 Audit

During a stage 1 audit, the auditor generally looks at the documentary evidence. This is sometimes called a *tabletop audit* or *document review audit*. Here, the auditor looks at the required process, policy, or procedure documents. The essential documents—such as the organizational information security policy, statement of applicability (SoA), and risk treatment plan—must be reviewed during a stage 1 audit.

You might wonder who all can attend a stage 1 audit. If you guessed the information security team, you would be correct. This team, on behalf of all the teams, showcases the defined policies and procedures. If there are any queries, they are handled by the security team.

Note   In some cases, the information security team won't be able to answer all the queries. In such scenarios, specific department stakeholders can be consulted.

The aim of the stage 1 audit is to ensure that your organization ISMS is in place and ready for the stage 2 audit.

Stage 2 Audit

The stage 2 audit is detail-oriented, and this formal audit is sometimes called a *compliance audit*. During this audit, the auditor must visit the organization's onsite office. The auditor first audits the information security team and then audits the remaining departments. The auditor reviews how the organization has implemented the security controls and whether they are effective and enough to secure the organization's information/assets.

The auditor also attempts to understand, from discussions with the auditees, why a certain method/tool was chosen as a security control. Hence, as an organization/team, you must be clear and confident about these choices.

After meeting with all the auditees/teams, the auditor prepares their findings and reports. Before they give the findings in front of management, they present it to the auditees to ensure that they agree on the noted findings.

Note   There should not be any major conformance issues in the audit report, as this will delay the certification process.

After the auditor reports the findings, they meet with the senior management to close the meeting. The auditor then presents the final report.

The process of preparing the report and sending it to the customers and certifying bodies may take a few days to a few weeks, depending on the situation and the external auditor. After the report is validated by the issuing authority/certifying body and after the organization passes the audit, the organization will be issued the audit certificate, which is valid for three years.

Stage 3 Audit

The stage 3 audit is the follow-up review and is generally called the *surveillance audit*. This audit is conducted on an annual basis to validate that the organization is maintaining the ISMS effectively and focusing on continual improvement. If the organization wants to increase or decrease the scope of the audit, that can be done during the surveillance audit and should be communicated to the certifying body well before the audit.

The next sections discuss the steps that can help you be audit-ready.

Step1: Understand the Context

This step will help you understand the business context, which in turns helps you understand the internal and external factors that affect the organization. Here you may note the points that can affect the outcome of the ISMS implementation. For example, an information asset can be an internal issue that affects the ISMS outcome.

Note   When identifying external issues, try using the PESTLE method. PESTLE stands for Political, Economic, Sociological, Technical, Legislative, and Environmental issues.

Step 2: Ensure Leadership Commitment

This is a simple yet very important step during the external audit. You need to have commitment from management throughout the project. They can participate, suggest an action, and assign roles and responsibilities.

Step 3: Plan the Audit

Planning is always important during the ISMS journey. Here, you can plan for your audit, control selection, manage risk, address the risk assessment results, and develop a risk treatment plan.

Tip   The communication plan can also be developed during this step and this communication plan will vary from company to company, depending on how complex it is and its various roles and responsibilities.

Step 4: Complete the Documentation

During this step, you need to define and implement the policies, procedures, and other record documents, such as review logs, network logs, and training records that are mandatory, as per the ISO 27001 standard guideline.

Step 5: Schedule Your Stage 1 Audit

At this point, you should have all the documents ready and the preparation complete. It's time to schedule the stage 1 audits with the external agency or auditor. You can get guidance from the auditor and clarify any doubts. This is your best chance to improve.

Step 6: Prepare Your Team

Now it's time to prepare your team for the audit. Discuss with the team and send an email if required about what they should expect to be asked and how to reply. The best way to reply to an auditor is to give real-life examples when you're asked for evidence.

Step 7: Close the Gaps

During this step, you need to close all the gaps or issues shared by the auditor during the stage 1 audit. By this time, the team will have confidence and will understand the audit cycle, as they already went through a stage 1 audit. Once the gaps are closed, they need to be sent back to the auditor for review. You need to obtain the auditor's approval that the issues have been resolved.

Step 8: Schedule Stage 2 Audit

This is the final step before receiving the ISO 27001 certificate. Schedule your stage 2 audit and relax. You have done everything you can, and you have the evidence that will be required by the auditor.

Step 9: Celebrate

This is an optional step, but your team has done well and earned this valuable certificate. Time to celebrate this achievement.

Best Practices

These external audit best practices help you address any compliance issues reported during the audit and help create more awareness for the team. Follow these best practices during the audit preparation stage:

- *Clearly understand the scope:* The scope must be clear to all participants who will be audited during the internal audit. For example, auditees and the senior management must be on the same page during the scope of an audit.

- *Focus on critical areas:* Pay attention to the critical areas of your business operations, which might have had ongoing open issues that you closed recently, a few months before the audit. Ensure that if any such areas are being audited, they remain complaint. Otherwise, non-compliance (NCs) could be reported in the audit.

- *Information security policy awareness:* All the teams must be aware of the information security policies. The information security team can hold awareness sessions in which they educate teams about the security policies.

- *Conduct mock audits:* This practice makes the team aware of which kinds of questions may come from the auditor. If the team is going for an ISMS audit for the first time, doing a mock audit is really helpful. The mock audit will make them familiar with the course of the audit and show them how to present evidence to the auditor.

- *Get approval on policy and procedure:* Organizations going for the certification audit for the first time must ensure that they perform checks on all the newly written policies and procedures to ensure they are reviewed and approved. Be sure to check that old defined policies has been reviewed for any changes.

- *Check software/tool expiration:* The organization should ensure that the software/tools used by the teams are licensed and that their expiration date is not before the audit.

- *Ensure traceability:* Teams should ensure that the business process or the part of the business process that they execute should be able to show end-to-end traceability. For example, any task in process should able to show a clear path of execution until its closure.

- *Keep manual execution to a minimum:* The organization should ensure that their business processes are executed by the help of software/tools/automation, as this will minimize the chance of security errors during execution. Having such tools helps the organization maintain its ISMS efficiently.

Audit Closure

This section covers how you mark an audit as closed. When the auditor has met all the department/stakeholders based on the audit schedule and has covered the complete audit scope, it's time to close the audit.

The audit was conducted to inspect your organization's security controls as per the defined policies and procedures. Hence, this audit helps you determine how well your business processes are helping to secure your organizational information/asset. The audit closure is the opportunity to understand the effectiveness of the implemented controls in your ISMS.

In general, most of you know when an audit is completed, which document you will receive as part of this phase. It is your audit report that will describe the audit's finding and the best practices you have implemented. This audit report will be presented during the audit closure report presentation.

Here are the key points that an auditor covers during the audit closure meeting.

- *Reiterate audit scope and objective:* The auditor will reiterate the audit scope and objective to ensure that he has covered the complete audit scope. For example, the objective of the audit was to evaluate how effectively the management system conforms with the requirements of the ISO 27001:2013 standard and the organization's policies. Also, the auditor will mention that the audit is conducted on a sampling basis.

- *Preliminary findings:* This is the key part of the closing meeting. The auditor explains all the findings in the audit to the team to make sure that the communication is clear and everyone understands it. The finding should be based on the available pieces of evidence.

- *Clarifications:* Clarifications about the findings can be done with the auditor during the preliminary and the final finding presentation. The team or management might clarify points and ask questions, if required. Someone on the team might not agree with the findings and be able to present other evidence to show that a given finding is not valid. This discussion is important, as it can impact the final audit report.

- *Acknowledgment:* The team acknowledges that they understand the findings.

- *Report:* The auditor communicates the timeline with the company to share the final audit report, as they must submit the report for verification with the certifying body.

By following these simple steps, the audit meeting can be closed. It seems like an easy job, right? (Irony intended.)

Audit Report

The final audit report was mentioned in the audit closure meeting section, previously. So, what is an audit report and how does it look?

An audit report, as its name suggests, is a detail-oriented report of the ISMS audit. The report structure may change according to the certifying body, but some of the important areas that it covers are described in the following sections.

Executive Summary

This section contains the objectives of an audit along with the company's details. Here's an example of the executive summary:

- The company has implemented ISMS in its software development, maintenance, support department. The company uses an AWS (Amazon Web Services) cloud for its application development and hosting requirements.

- The ISMS objectives, along with its policies, were verified with reference to the ISMS Manual v1.0 dated (date here).

- Information Security Policy v1.0, ISMS-Roles, Responsibilities, and Authorities v1.2 dated (date here).

- Risk Assessment Procedure v1.0 dated (date here), Statement of Applicability v1.1 dated (date here).

- The only control excluded is A.14.2.7, outsourced software development, as the organization does not use outsourced software development services.

- All candidates went through pre-employment checks as per the Reference Check Policy. Confidentiality forms are part of the employment terms. All employees must give an undertaking at the time of issue of any company assets.

- As the company uses cloud services, all IT server infrastructure is on the cloud. The IT infrastructure in the facility includes laptops, fileserver, router/firewall, LAN switches, and Internet links.

- The development, staging, and the live environments are on the cloud.

- Firewall alerts/alarms are configured to trigger an email to the IT manager.

- The software development methodology used is a mixture of SDLC and Agile. The technology used is JAVA, J2EE, Node.Js, Machine Learning, and Big Data.

- Patch management is automatic for Windows laptops and manually done for servers. Vulnerability management is done by scanning systems once a month using Nessus.

- The applicable legal, statutory, and regulatory requirements have been identified and documented in the Legal Authorities Register v1.0 dated (date here) and the organization has implemented mechanisms to ensure compliance.

- The internal audits are conducted once a year as per policy. The last internal audit was conducted on (month and year). All findings of the audit have been closed with appropriate RCA. The next round of internal audits will be performed on (month and year).

- The management reviews are conducted once every six months as per policy. The last management review was conducted on (date here). The next management review is scheduled for (month and year).

Note   The Executive Summary points mentioned here are for understanding purposes only; the description can be modified based on the organization or industry.

SWOT Analysis

In this section, the auditor writes down the Strength, Weakness, Opportunity, and Threats (SWOT) observed during the stage 2 audit.

For example, the SWOT analysis can be:

- **Strengths**
  - Leadership commitment toward information security
  - Expertise and strong domain understanding
- **Weaknesses**
  - No significant weaknesses observed
- **Opportunities**
  - ISMS monitoring mechanisms may be improved
  - Coverage of documented operating procedures may improve
- **Threats**
  - Adverse economic and political conditions in the client countries
  - Any adverse changes in the outsourcing policies of client companies

Scope Description Control by Control

The score descriptions are universal to all management systems and cannot be customized by the auditor. This ensures consistency of interpretation and standardization of audit results worldwide. The scores provided to your organization are for benchmarking purposes only and are based on the audit team's evaluation. Here the auditor will mention whether you meet all the controls and share the ratings for each control.

Finding Summary

In this section, the auditor will share a summary of the key findings that were issued during the stage 2 audit. The findings are categorized as Minor or Major. If the auditor identified any opportunities for improvements, that can also be noted in this section.

Evidence Summary

In this section, the management system evidence that the auditor audited can be summarized. The auditor is supposed to share their detailed evidence summary based on the audit.

Lead Auditor Recommendation

Here is where the final recommendation part comes in. The auditor will write her recommendation about whether the company should be awarded a certificate or not. For example, "the management system conforms with the audit criteria and can be considered effective in assuring that objectives will be met. Certification is therefore recommended."

Front Page

Figure 9-1 shows a snapshot of the audit report front page, which covers some basic details that were not discussed in the previous sections.

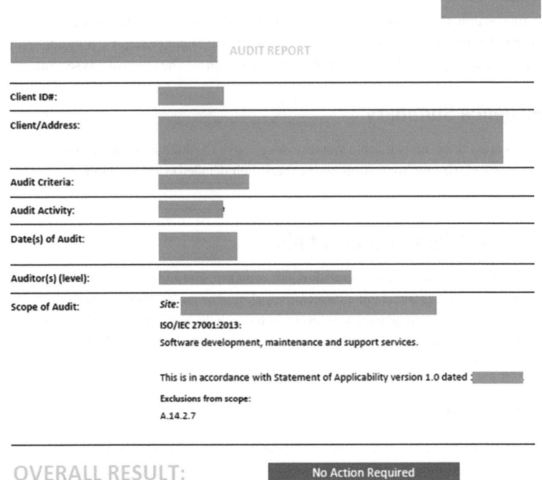

Figure 9-1. *Sample audit report front page showing basic details*

Summary

This chapter taught you the external audit process, including how you need to prepare and manage the audit. You also learned about the best practices that can be followed to smoothen the audit pace. At the end of this chapter, you learned about the audit closure and important points to remember so you can close the audit successfully.

CHAPTER 10

Continual Improvement

"Continuous improvement is the only cultural value that could unify an organization as large and diverse as ours."

—Anonymous

This final chapter discusses continual improvement. Is continual improvement needed when you have implemented the ISO 27001 standard controls and have been audited/certified by an external certifying body? The fact is, your duty is not over once you are certified. Many organizations don't focus on further improvements or stop adding to the scope areas that were not identified in earlier implementations once they achieve certification. They assume that the normal controls have been implemented and this will help safeguard their company's information security.

The *plan, do, check, and act principle,* mentioned in the previous chapter, states that your focus should always be on checking and acting. This will help you maintain the information security management system that you established after so much effort and time.

How does "check and act" help? Regular checks on security controls and their associated policies and standard operating procedures are the key. You must remember that there is no shortcut to achieving this. These checks will tell you where you still have gaps. Once you identify the gaps, it is time to act. That means working on improvement, which is a never-ending cycle.

Let's first consider where you'll learn about possible areas for improvement.

© Abhishek Chopra, Mukund Chaudhary 2020
A. Chopra and M. Chaudhary, *Implementing an Information Security Management System,*
https://doi.org/10.1007/978-1-4842-5413-4_10

Areas of Improvement

Many organizations struggle in this area, as they don't know how to identify the improvement areas or who will work on them. Once the external audit is completed, you receive the audit report. It tells you about the gaps/improvement areas and the organization's strengths.

Hence, you can start from that report and identify the areas of improvement.

Monthly KPIs/Reports

These monthly reports always have something to tell you about the health of the system/controls and whether there are areas of concern. Once you start analyzing them, you'll recognize consistent improvement areas. This is the fastest way to identify improvements, as you get these reports on a monthly or bi-weekly basis. Although it may not be possible to identify improvements every month, these reports provide a path to doing so if needed.

Employee Observations

Employees use the system daily and usually observe everything around them. They can share issues they observe, which you might never think about. Their eyes can see which you cannot.

Employee incident reports are one of the important sources of improvement areas. These reports show loopholes in the system, whether they are small or big.

Note   All employees, including new employees who joined the organization recently, must be made aware of the practice to report incidents whenever they observe them.

New employees bring experience from previous employers in the way of best practices, tools/technologies, and so on, which they think could be followed at your company. Providing new employees the ways and means to share this kind of information to the security team is important. This should be included on the improvement tracker form.

Tip   Employees whose ideas for improvement are incorporated could be awarded in some way. This might motivate other employees to share their ideas, which in turn could benefit the organization more than the reward paid to the employees.

Periodic Internal Audits

As important as the external audit is, periodic internal audits are equally important in terms of identifying improvement areas. The external audit focuses on continual improvements only and not on finding faults with the people/system. The periodic audit cycle also tells you what is working and what is not, whether it's time to change the process or something that has not been followed for a long time. These gaps could be due to many different reasons. If you drill down to the important root causes, these are likely the improvement areas.

Management Review Meetings

During management review meetings, management/steering committee members will often share areas of improvement when they're reviewing the business objectives/goals. Any improvement identified in this setting should be implemented.

Customers/Clients

Looking critically at your clients' processes, tools, and systems, you could come to understand any area that poses challenges in safeguarding client information. If you drill down to the root cause of these issues (whether you lack skill and or you have not used such tools/systems before), you'll see this is an important area of learning.

New Tools/Technology

When a new, pertinent technology/tool is launched in the market, it becomes important to explore it. You need to determine whether it would be useful to the organizations you serve.

Your clients may expect you to have experience with these new technologies. Hence, your organization must review them on a timely basis and determine whether they are useful to invest time and money in them, in order to keep the organization on par with its competitors. If you are investing time and resources in this approach, it becomes part of the improvement implementation.

Regulatory/Governmental Laws

Any law mandated by the government must be adhered to; this cannot be avoided. You must consider not only the local laws but also any international or country laws where your clients are based. Otherwise, they cannot accept the products or services provided by the organization. Hence, whenever new laws are published, they must be analyzed. Any security controls implemented around them to safeguard information must be identified as part of the improvement tracker.

There could be many more sources from where you can get the improvement areas identified. This list is a starting point to help you to think about and find sources. Your long-term goal should be to maintain and improve the information security management system to the benefit of the organization.

Execution Plan

Once you have identified your actionable improvement areas, it is time to go ahead and implement them.

The main responsibility of the information security team is to collate all the gaps/ improvement areas on the improvement tracker in order of priority and target dates. It would be difficult to work on all the improvements at the same time. Because of that, it's better and recommended to sort them in order of priority and based on the ones that could affect the business objectives/goals and might impact the business's reputation.

Once the improvement tracker is updated, it must be reviewed with management, as it's possible that more improvements could be added or removed, or the priorities could be changed.

The tracker/plan should forecast out about six months. Longer than that and it might lose importance or visibility. Issues are easier to track when they have a shorter duration. It is important to track the progress of each improvement and communicate the status to all on a periodic/planned basis. If there are issues, discuss them with the stakeholders as soon as possible, so that they don't grow to become a bigger issue later in front of management.

Pilot the Improvement First

It's very important to test-pilot the improvement first, as you cannot safely implement an improvement before testing it, especially if it is related to tools or technology. You need to know its impact on the system or the users. Plan a pilot, execute it on a small group of users or systems in a controlled environment, record the results, and carefully analyze them.

Once the test passes without incident, you can roll it out in a planned manner. It's still advisable to monitor it for few more weeks or a month, to verify that everything is running smoothly. Users must know that the rollout is happening so they can report all problems or incidents to the information security department. The goal is to rectify the problems as soon as possible so there's no disruption in business processes.

Measure Success

The success of the implementation is also measured in terms of which benefits an organization has achieved, and this must be regularly communicated to the management/steering committee. Most improvement areas take time and money to fix, and management is interested in knowing the benefits of those changes or what ROIs (return on investments) are attained.

Hence, the information security team must collate numbers from their improvement tracker and present them (with the benefits achieved) to management. This presentation can be done quarterly or twice a year, as there should be a good amount of progress at those intervals.

During this time if you do not make progress on some of the improvement areas, the information security team should take the blame. Don't try to blame other members from various teams who were supporting you. Even though it is the responsibility of everybody to give their efforts toward securing the information of the organization, the responsibility of implementation is still on the information security team, as they are the driving force making the improvements.

Figure 10-1 shows a sample improvement plan tracker template.

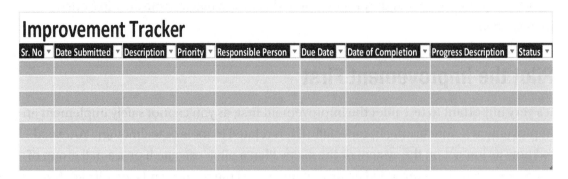

Improvement Tracker

Sr. No	Date Submitted	Description	Priority	Responsible Person	Due Date	Date of Completion	Progress Description	Status

Figure 10-1. *Sample improvement plan tracker template*

You should refrain from the blame game, as this can spoil your relationship with other teams in the organization. This is not good in the long run, as the information security team might not get the support needed to implement new improvements. Instead, focus on creating a win-win situation, with all employees working for the benefit of the organization.

Organizations can create, customize, and tailor their tracker templates. They can be created and maintained quarterly/half-yearly/yearly. It will help the implementation team to know how many improvements were implemented during a certain period and how much time on average it takes to implement one improvement. This data will help the teams analyze the progress made so far.

Performing Regular Audits/Reviews

After implementing the improvements on a regular basis, the audit becomes an important exercise, as it will also help you assess whether improvements have helped the organization and will continue to do so in the long run. You want to determine whether it's sustainable and whether these improvements have given birth to new opportunities for new improvements.

The audit also becomes important because it allows you to look at the practices followed by your vendors who work for your organization. These vendors deliver secure products and services to your organization clients/customers. Hence, regular audits will help your vendors identify their gaps, many of which they might not be aware.

From the vendor compliance perspective, it also becomes important to do regular vendor risk-assessment exercises. These exercises will help you ascertain whether the security controls implemented by the vendor are enough to protect not only your organization information but also your clients'/customers' information. Any information security breach, however small, could impact the organization's brand or image.

When your project or contract with the vendor is completed, and your organization no longer needs the vendor's services, you need to conduct an audit at the vendor site to ensure that their systems do not have you or your client's your confidential information stored on their systems/machines or in documents on paper.

This should be part of your contact with the vendor—that your organization has the right to conduct an audit/review on a regular basis. Also, if your organization finds any discrepancies in the processes or the terms of the contract are not fulfilled by the vendor as mentioned in the contract, you have a right to conduct an audit. This will remind the vendor that they need to abide by the terms and conditions of the contract. They then understand that any compliance issues could lead to a penalty or contract cancellation.

Audits could also become important at your organization. Your client/customer might request an audit of your organization processes or office premises before awarding the project/contract to your organization, in order to check whether enough security controls are implemented to support them. Your client could also do those audits midway through the project if they find discrepancies in your processes in terms of securing their information. Hence, to be ready for such scenarios, it is important that your organization conduct internal audits/checks reviews regularly.

Summary

This last chapter focused on the importance of identifying ongoing improvement areas after the external audit certification exercise. It covered the various sources you can use to identify needed improvements, what your execution plan should be to implement the improvements, and why you need to conduct regular audits/reviews. All these steps will help maintain the information security management system in your organization and help you attain greater benefits in the long run.

This chapter concludes the book. It's our hope that this book has not only given you theoretical knowledge, but also provided many tips for managing your ISO 27001 audit successfully.

Index

A

© Abhishek Chopra, Mukund Chaudhary 2020
A. Chopra and M. Chaudhary, *Implementing an Information Security Management System*,
https://doi.org/10.1007/978-1-4842-5413-4

T

Printed in the United States
By Bookmasters